The
Quotable
Lover

Also in the *Quotable* Series:

The Quotable Writer by William A. Gordon
The Quotable Historian by Alan Axelrod
The Quotable Woman by Carol Turkington
The Quotable Executive by John Woods

The Quotable Lover

Words of Wisdom from Shakespeare,
Emily Dickinson, John Keats,
Robert Burns, and More

CAROL A. TURKINGTON

McGraw-Hill

New York   San Francisco   Washington, D.C.   Auckland   Bogotá
Caracas   Lisbon   London   Madrid   Mexico City   Milan
Montreal   New Delhi   San Juan   Singapore
Sydney   Tokyo   Toronto

McGraw-Hill

A Division of The McGraw-Hill Companies

1 2 3 4 5 6 7 8 9 0   DOC/DOC   0 9 8 7 6 5 4 3 2 1 0

ISBN 0-07-136064-6

Printed and bound by R. R. Donnelley & Sons Company.

McGraw-Hill books are available at special quantity discounts to use as premiums and sales promotions, or for use in corporate training programs. For more information, please write to the Director of Special Sales, Professional Publishing, McGraw-Hill, 2 Penn Plaza, New York, NY 10121-2298. Or contact your local bookstore.

This publication is designed to provide accurate and authoritative information in regard to the subject matter covered. It is sold with the understanding that neither the author nor the publisher is engaged in rendering legal, accounting, or other professional service. If legal advice or other expert assistance is required, the services of a competent professional person should be sought. —*From a Declaration of Principles jointly adopted by a Committee of the American Bar Association and a Committee of Publishers.*

 This book is printed on recycled, acid-free paper containing a minimum of 50% recycled, de-inked fiber.

☙ Contents ☙

v

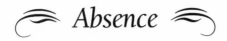 Absence

When my self is not with you, it is nowhere.
> ━HELOISE, ca 1098–1164,
> letter to Peter Abelard

Absence makes the heart grow fonder.
> ━SEXTUS PROPERTIUS,
> *Elegies* (54 B.C.– A.D. 2)

Moonlight, a wood fire, my own good lamp. What can I complain about? Only the absence of those I love.
> ━COLETTE,
> letter, January 3, 1928

He is gone, who knew the music of my soul.
> ━HSUEH T'AO, 768–831,
> *Weaving Love Knots*

It takes time for the absent to assume their true shape in our thoughts.
> ━COLETTE,
> *Sido*, 1929

Absence diminishes commonplace passions and increases great ones, as the wind extinguishes candles and kindles fire.
> ━DUC DE LA ROCHEFOUCAULD,
> *Maximes*, 1678

My life will be sour grapes and ashes without you.
> ━DAISY ASHFORD,
> *The Young Visitors*, 1919

I am shattered, numb, as though after a long orgy; I miss you terribly. There is an immense void in my heart.

   ➤ GUSTAVE FLAUBERT,
      letter to Louise Colet, August 7, 1846

Love reckons hours for months, and days for years; every little absence is an age.

   ➤ JOHN DRYDEN,
      "Amphitryon," 1690

Our hours in love have wings; in absence, crutches.

   ➤ COLLEY CIBBER,
      Xerxes, **1699**

Absence becomes the greatest Presence.

   ➤ MAY SARTON,
      "Difficult Scene," *The Lion and the Rose*, **1948**

Absence is to love what wind is to a fire; it puts out the little, it kindles the great.

   ➤ ROGER DE BUSSY-RABUTIN,
      Histoire Amoureuse des Gaules, **1868**

Absence on Love effects the same
As winds oppos'd to fire
Extinguishes a feeble Flame
And blows a great one higher

   ➤ ANNE FINCH,
      "On Absence," *Miscellany Poems, Written by a Lady*, **1713**

Absence, that common cure of love.

   ➤ MIGUEL DE CERVANTES,
      Don Quixote, **1605**

(See also *Loneliness*)

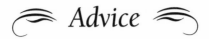 Advice

A woman seldom asks advice before she has bought her wedding clothes.
— JOSEPH ADDISON,
The Spectator, September 4, 1712

In matters of religion and matrimony I never give any advice; because I will not have anybody's torments in this world or the next laid to my charge.
— LORD CHESTERFIELD,
letter to Arthur Charles Stanhope, October 12, 1765

 Affairs

You know, of course, that the Tasmanians, who never committed adultery, are now extinct.
— W. SOMERSET MAUGHAM,
The Bread-Winner, 1930

A mistress kept at first is sweet,
And joys to do the merry feat;
But bastards come and hundreds gone,
You'll wish you'd left her charms alone,
Such breeding hussies are a pest,
A neighbour's wife is far the best.
— ANONYMOUS,
"The Pearl," 1879–1880

Reading someone else's newspaper is like sleeping with someone else's wife. Nothing seems to be precisely in the right place, and when you find what you are looking for, it is not clear then how to respond to it.

➤MALCOLM BRADBURY,
Stepping Westward, 1975

I'm old-fashioned. I don't believe in extra-marital relationships. I think people should mate for life, like pigeons or Catholics.

➤WOODY ALLEN,
Manhattan, 1979

I say I don't sleep with married men, but what I mean is that I don't sleep with happily married men.

➤BRITT EKLAND, attributed, 1980,
in *Like a Fish Needs a Bicycle* by Anne Stibbs, ed., 1992

I've looked on a lot of women with lust. I've committed adultery in my heart many times. This is something that God recognizes I will do—and I have done it—and God forgives me for it.

➤JIMMY CARTER,
Playboy, November 1976

Cuckoldry is an essential appendage of wedlock; your shadow does not follow you more closely or naturally. When you hear the three words: "He is married," add: "Therefore, he is, has been, will or may be cuckolded." Do this, and no one will ever accuse you of faulty logic.

➤FRANCOIS RABELAIS,
Gargantua and Pantagruel, 1534

People who are so dreadfully devoted to their wives are so apt, from mere habit, to get devoted to other people's wives as well.

➤JANE CARLYLE, 1801,
quoted in *Hammer and Tongues* by Michele Brown and Ann O'Connor, 1986

When you marry your mistress, you automatically create a
vacancy.
—JAMES GOLDSMITH,
The Sunday Times, March 12, 1989

I had three concubines, who in three diverse properties diversely
excelled. One, the merriest; another the wiliest; the third, the holi-
est harlot in my realm, as one whom no man could get out of the
church lightly to any place but it were his bed.
—Edward IV,
in THOMAS MORE, *The History of Richard III*, composed about
1513

Adultery is a meanness and a stealing, a taking away from someone
what should be theirs, a great selfishness, and surrounded and
guarded by lies lest it should be found out. And out of the meanness and selfishness and lying flow love and joy and peace beyond
anything that can be imagined.
—ROSE MACAULAY,
The Towers of Trebizond, 1956

No adultery is bloodless.
—NATALIE GINZBURG,
The City and the House, 1985

If you bed people of below-stairs class, they will go to the papers.
—JANE CLARK,
Daily Telegraph, May 31, 1994

Adultery is the application of democracy to love.
—H. L. MENCKEN,
Book of Burlesques, 1920

There is nothing better for the spirit or body than a love affair. It
elevates thoughts and flattens stomachs.
—BARBARA HOWARD,
Laughing All the Way, 1973

Sara could commit adultery at one end and weep for her sins at the other, and enjoy both operations at once.

—Joyce Cary,
The Horse's Mouth, 1944

(See also *Seduction*)

Affection

One is apt to think of people's affection as a fixed quantity, instead of a sort of moving sea with tide always going out or coming in, but still fundamentally there.

—Freya Stark,
The Coast of Incense, 1953

Trust in my affection for you. Tho' I may not display it exactly in the way you like and expect it, it is not therefore less deep and sincere.

—Anna Jameson, 1833,
quoted in by G. H. Needler, 1939

My affection hath an unknown bottom, like the bay of Portugal.

—William Shakespeare,
As You Like It, 1599

(See also *Enduring Love, Falling in Love, First Love, Love, Love vs. Like, True Love, Young Love*)

 *Age*

Oh, who could have foretold
That the heart grows old?
— WILLIAM BUTLER YEATS,
  "A Song," 1919

So we'll go no more a-roving
So late into the night,
Though the heart be still as loving,
And the moon be still as bright.

For the sword outwears its sheath,
And the soul wears out the breast,
And the heart must pause to breathe,
And love itself have rest.
— LORD BYRON,
  "So We'll Go No More A-Roving," 1817

Age cannot wither her, nor custom stale
Her infinite variety.
— WILLIAM SHAKESPEARE,
  Antony and Cleopatra, 1607

It's never too late to have a fling,
For Autumn is just as nice as Spring,
And it's never too late to fall in love.
— SANDY WILSON,
  "It's Never Too Late to Fall in Love," 1954

The age of a woman doesn't mean a thing. The best tunes are played on the oldest fiddles.

— SIGMUND ENGEL,
   Newsweek, July 4, 1949

As a white candle
In a holy place,
So is the beauty
Of an aged face.

— JOSEPH CAMPBELL,
   "The Old Woman (1881–1944)"

Believe me, if all those endearing young charms
Which I gaze on so fondly today,
Were to change by tomorrow and fleet in my arms,
Like fairy gifts fading away,
Thou should'st still be ador'd as this moment thou art,
Let thy loveliness fade as it will,
And around the dear ruin each wish of my heart
Would entwine itself verdantly still.

— THOMAS MOORE,
   "Believe Me, If All Those Endearing Young Charms," *Irish Melodies*, 1834

If grass can grow through cement, love can find you at every time in your life.

— CHER,
   The Times, May 30, 1998

How unnatural the imposed view, imposed by a puritanical ethos, that passionate love belongs only to the young, that people are dead from the neck down by the time they are forty, and that any deep feeling, any passion after that age, is either ludicrous or revolting.

— MAY SARTON,
   Journal of a Solitude, 1973

I have everything I had 20 years ago, except now it's all lower.

—GYPSY ROSE LEE,
  Newsweek, September 16, 1968

There are some things (like first love and one's reviews) at which a woman in her middle years does not care to look too closely.

—STELLA GIBBONS,
  foreword, *Cold Comfort Farm*, 1932

Grow old along with me!
The best is yet to be,
The last of life, for which the first was made.

—ROBERT BROWNING,
  Rabbi Ben Ezra, 1864

No spring, nor summer beauty hath such grace,
As I have seen in one autumnal face.

—JOHN DONNE,
  "The Autumnal," c 1600

Will you still need me, will you still feed me,
When I'm sixty four?

—JOHN LENNON and PAUL MCCARTNEY,
  "When I'm Sixty Four," 1967

A woman would rather visit her own grave than the place where she had been young and beautiful after she is aged and ugly.

—CORRA MAY HARRIS,
  Eva's Second Husband, 1910

There are few things that we so unwillingly give up, even in advanced age, as the supposition that we still have the power of ingratiating ourselves with the fair sex.

—SAMUEL JOHNSON,
  quoted in *Johnsonian Miscellanies* by George Birkbeck, ed.,
   1897

One is never too old for romance.
— INGRID BERGMAN,
Sunday Mirror, May 5, 1974

Darling, I am growing old,
Silver threads among the gold.
— EBEN E. REXFORD,
"Silver Threads Among the Gold," 1873

When you are old and grey and full of sleep,
And nodding by the fire, take down this book
And slowly read and dream of the soft look
Your eyes had once, and of their shadows deep.
— W. B. YEATS,
"When You Are Old," 1893

(See also *Mature Love*)

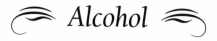

Alcohol

There is wan thing, an' on'y wan thing, to be said in favour iv
dhrink, an
that is that it has caused manny a lady to be loved that otherwise
might've died single.
— FINLEY PETER DUNNE,
Mr. Dooley Says, 1910

(See also *Wine*)

Alone

Once you have lived with another, it is a great torture to have to live alone.

—Carson McCullers,
The Ballad of the Sad Cafe, 1953

When love is out of your life, you're through in a way. Because while it is there it's like a motor that's going, you have such vitality to do things, big things, because love is goosing you all the time.

—Fanny Brice,
quoted in *The Fabulous Fanny* by Norman Katkov, 1952

A woman without a man cannot meet a man, any man, of any age, without thinking, even if it's for a half-second, Perhaps this is *the* man.

—Doris Lessing,
The Golden Notebook, 1962

When I'm alone, I can sleep crossways in bed without an argument.

—Zsa Zsa Gabor,
on being between marriages,
Family Weekly, May 7, 1976

Even quarrels with one's husband are preferable to the ennui of a solitary existence.

—Elizabeth Patterson Bonaparte,
quoted in *The Life and Letters of Madame Bonaparte* by
Eugene L. Didier, 1879

It makes me wince when I hear Mum refer to me as "her independent daughter." (Query: why does the word "independent" sound more like "lesbian" or "on the shelf" or "no idea how to hold down a relationship" or "a complete disappointment to me in every way" when uttered by a mother?)

— ARABELLA WEIR,
   Does My Bum Look Big In This?, 1997

At Christmas little children sing and merry bells jingle,
The cold winter air makes our hands and faces tingle
And happy families go to church and cheerily they mingle
And the whole business is unbelievably dreadful, if you're single.

— WENDY COPE,
   "A Christmas Poem," 1992

Marriage may often be a stormy lake, but celibacy is almost always a muddy horsepond.

— THOMAS LOVE PEACOCK,
   Melincourt, 1817

But earthlier happy is the rose distilled,
Than that which is withering on the virgin thorn
Grows, lives, and dies, in single blessedness.

— WILLIAM SHAKESPEARE,
   A Midsummer Night's Dream, 1595

If I am to disclose to you that I should prefer if I follow the inclination of my nature, it is this: beggar-woman and single, far rather than queen and married!

— ELIZABETH I,
   attributed reply to an imperial envoy (1563)
   Queen Elizabeth I by J. E. Neale, 1979

(See also *Loneliness*)

Anniversary

She had celebrated her silver wedding and renewed her intimacy with her husband by waltzing with him to Mr. Powers's accompaniment.

—JAMES JOYCE,
Dubliners, 1914

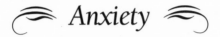

Anxiety

Love looks forward, hate looks back, anxiety has eyes all over its head.

—MIGNON MCLAUGHLIN,
The Neurotic's Notebook, 1963

Anxiety is love's greatest killer. It makes others feel as you might when a drowning man holds on to you. You want to save him, but you know he will strangle you with his panic.

—ANAIS NIN,
The Diary of Anais Nin, 1974

Appearance

Why not be oneself? That is the whole secret of a successful appearance. If one is a greyhound why try to look like a Pekinese?

—EDITH SITWELL,
"Why I Look As I Do," *Collected Poems*, 1954

Is it too much to ask that women be spared the daily struggle for superhuman beauty in order to offer it to the caresses of a subhumanly ugly mate?

    —GERMAINE GREER,
       The Female Eunuch, 1970

When the heart is in love, beauty is of no account.

    —Afghanistan proverb

Only the really plain people know about love—the very fascinating ones try so hard to create an impression that they soon exhaust their talents.

    —KATHARINE HEPBURN,
       Look, February 18, 1958

Never choose your women or your linen by candlelight. (Originally: Choose not a woman, nor linnen clothe by the candle)

    —J. SANFORDE,
       Garden of Pleasure, 1573

After forty a woman has to choose between losing her figure or her face. My advice is to keep your face, and stay sitting down.

    —BARBARA CARTLAND,
       The Times, October 6, 1993

(See also *Attraction, Beauty*)

Applause

If nothing else, there's applause…like waves of love pouring over the footlights.

    —Eve Harrington in *All About Eve*
       by JOSEPH L. MANKIEWICZ, 1950

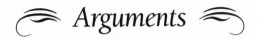

Arguments

The more I love, the more I quarrel.

— Marguerite d'Angouleme,
Dixains, 1547

Sir, I have quarrelled with my wife; and a man who has quarrelled with his wife is absolved from all duty to his country.

— Thomas Love Peacock,
Nightmare Abbey, 1818

The concept of two people living together for 25 years without having a cross word suggests a lack of spirit only to be admired in sheep.

— A. P. Herbert,
News Chronicle, 1940

A married couple are well suited when both partners usually feel the need for a quarrel at the same time.

— Jean Rostand,
Le Mariage, 1927

Never go to bed mad. Stay up and fight.

— Phyllis Diller,
Phyllis Diller's Housekeeping Hints, 1966

Attraction

In the factory we make cosmetics; in the store we sell hope.

— Charles Revson,
Fire and Ice, 1976

(i do not know what it is about you that closes
and opens; only something in me understands
the voice of your eyes is deeper than all roses)
nobody, not even the rain, has such small hands

✎ E.E. CUMMINGS,
   "somewhere I have never travelled," 1931

When I find a woman attractive, I have nothing at all to say. I simply watch her smile. Intellectuals take apart her face in order to
explain it bit by bit, but they no longer see the smile.

✎ ANTOINE DE SAINT-EXUPERY,
   Pilote de Guerre, 1942

What else do they want in life but to be as attractive as possible to
men? Do not all their trimmings and cosmetics have this end in
view, and all their baths, fittings, creams, scents, as well—and all
those arts of making up, painting and fashioning the face, eyes and
skin? And by what other sponsor are they better recommended to
men than by folly?

✎ ERASMUS,
   In Praise of Folly, 1509

Tisn't beauty, so to speak, nor good talk necessarily. It's just It.
Some women'll stay in a man's memory if they once walked down
a street.

✎ RUDYARD KIPLING,
   Traffics and Discoveries, 1904

Sex appeal isn't just straight teeth, a square jaw and a solid torso.
Look at me. I'm sixty-three and first thing in the morning I have a
face like a woollen mat. And yet I am the most desirable man in the
world. Indeed, if I put my mind to it I am sure I could pass the
supreme test and lure Miss Taylor away from Mr. Burton.

✎ NOEL COWARD,
   quoted in *The Wit of Noel Coward* by Dick Richards, 1968

She gave me a smile I could feel in my hip pocket.

━RAYMOND CHANDLER,
　Farewell My Lovely, 1940

The more serious the face, the more beautiful the smile.

━FRANÇOIS-RENE CHATEAUBRIAND,
　Memoires d'Outre-Tombe, 1849–1850

Power is the great aphrodisiac.

━HENRY KISSINGER,
　in *The New York Times*, 1971

 *Bachelors*

In Mexico, a bachelor is a man who can't play the guitar.

━LILLIAN DAY,
　Kiss and Tell, 1931

Bachelors know more about women than married men. If they did
not they would be married, too.

━H. L. MENCKEN,
　Chrestomathy, 1949

Summer bachelors, like summer breezes, are never as cool as they
pretend to be.

━NORA EPHRON,
　New York Post, August 22, 1965

Bachelors know all about parties. In fact, a good bachelor is a living, breathing party all by himself.

━P. J. O'ROURKE,
　The Bachelor Home Companion, 1987

A bachelor is a man who can take a nap on top of a bedspread.
— MARCELENE COX,
Ladies Home Journal, 1949

 *Beauty*

Beauty more than bitterness makes the heart break.
— SARA TEASDALE,
"Vignettes Overseas: Capri," *Rivers to the Sea*, 1915

A woman of so shining loveliness
that men threshed corn at midnight by a tress,
A little stolen tress.
— W. B. YEATS,
"The Secret Rose," 1899

Oh, thou art fairer than the evening air
Clad in the beauty of a thousand stars.
— CHRISTOPHER MARLOWE,
The Tragical History of Doctor Faustus,1604

Who is she that looketh forth as the morning, fair as the moon,
clear as the sun, and terrible as an army with banners?
— Song of Solomon

I love all beauteous things,
I seek and adore them;
God hath no better praise,
And man in his hasty days
Is honored for them.
— ROBERT BRIDGES,
Shorter Poems, 1890

The most deeply moving element in the contemplation of beauty is the element of loss. We desire to hold; but the sunset melts into the night, and the secret of the painting on the wall can never be the secret of the buyer.

→ PAMELA HANSFORD JOHNSON,
Catherine Carter, 1958

For she was beautiful—her beauty made
The bright world dim, and everything beside
Seemed like the fleeting image of a shade.

→ PERCY BYSSHE SHELLEY,
"The Witch of Atlas," 1870

For beauty being the best of all we know
Sums up the unsearchable and secret aims
Of nature.

→ ROBERT BRIDGES,
"The Growth of Love," 1890

Beauty is truth, truth beauty—that is all
Ye know on earth, and all ye need to know

→ JOHN KEATS,
"Ode on a Grecian Urn," 1820

A thing of beauty is a joy for ever:
Its loveliness increases
It will never
Pass into nothingness.

→ JOHN KEATS,
Endymion, 1818

One frequently only finds out how really beautiful a really beautiful woman is after considerable acquaintance with her; and the rule applies to Niagara Falls, to majestic mountains, and to mosques—especially to mosques.

→ MARK TWAIN,
The Innocents Abroad, 1869

O, she doth teach the torches to burn bright.
It seems she hangs upon the cheek of night
Like a rich jewel in an Ethiop's ear;
Beauty too rich for use, for earth too dear.
> ➤WILLIAM SHAKESPEARE,
> *Romeo and Juliet*, 1595

Shall I compare thee to a summer's day?
Thou art more lovely and more temperate.
> ➤WILLIAM SHAKESPEARE,
> *Sonnet XVIII*, 1589

A witty woman is a treasure; a witty beauty is a power.
> ➤GEORGE MEREDITH,
> *Diana of the Crossways*, 1885

Beauty is the lover's gift.
> ➤WILLIAM CONGREVE,
> *The Way of the World*, 1700

Yet beauty, though injurious, hath strange power,
After offence returning, to regain
Love once possessed.
> ➤JOHN MILTON,
> *Samson Agonistes*, 1979

She is not fair to outward view
As many maidens be;
Her loveliness I never knew
Until she smiled on me.
> ➤HARTLEY COLERIDGE,
> "She Is Not Fair," 1833

Beauty's but skin deep.
> ➤JOHN DAVIES OF HEREFORD,
> *A Select Second Husband for Sir Thomas Overburie's Wife*, 1616

Handsome is as handsome does.

➼ OLIVER GOLDSMITH,
The Vicar of Wakefield, 1766

What woman whose beauty time has at last ravaged can hear without tears the song that her lover once sung to her?

➼ MME. DE STÄEL,
Lettres sur les ouvrages et le caractere de J. J. Rousseau, 1788

She walks in beauty, like the night
Of cloudless climes and starry skies.

➼ LORD BYRON,
"She Walks in Beauty," 1815

Fair is my love, and cruel as she's fair,
Her brow shades frowns,
although her eyes are sunny.

➼ SAMUEL DANIEL,
Sonnets to Delia, 1592

(See also *Appearance*)

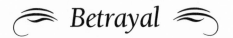

Betrayal

Yet each man kills the thing he loves,
By each let this be heard,
Some do it with a bitter look,
Some with a flattering word.
The coward does it with a kiss,
The brave man with a sword!

➼ OSCAR WILDE,
"The Ballad of Reading Gaol," 1898

You know what man really desires? One of two things: to find someone who is so stupid that he can lie to her, or to love someone so much that she can lie to him.

➤ DJUNA BARNES,
  Nightwood, 1936

Believing that a girl will wait is like jumping with a parachute packed by someone else.

➤ NIKOLAI CHEPIK,
  from diary of Soviet farm boy who died in action in
    Afghanistan,
  The New York Times, January 16, 1985

It was the man I deceived the most that I loved the most.

➤ MARGUERITE DURAS,
  Practicalities, 1990

She was never attracted to anyone young and whole-hearted and free— she was, in fact, a congenital poacher.

➤ RADCLYFFE HALL,
  The Well of Loneliness, 1928

I saw this thing turn, like a flower, once picked, turning petals into bright knives in your hand. And it was so much desired, so lovely, that your fingers will not loosen, and you have only disbelief that this, of all you have ever known, should have the possibility of pain.

➤ NADINE GORDIMER,
  The Lying Days, 1953

When one loves a certain way, even betrayals become unimportant.

➤ COLETTE,
  Claudine and Annie, 1903

Betrayal can only happen if you love.

➤ JOHN LE CARRE,
  A Perfect Spy, 1986

Sure men were born to lie, and women to believe them.
—JOHN GAY,
  The Beggar's Opera, 1728

If only one could tell true love from false love as one can tell mushrooms from toadstools.
—KATHERINE MANSFIELD,
  Journal of Katherine Mansfield, 1930

(See also *Divorce, Heartbreak, Parting*)

Bisexuality

I came to live in a country I love; some people label me a defector. I have loved men and women in my life; I've been labeled "the bisexual defector." Want to know another secret? I'm even ambidextrous. I don't like labels. Just call me Martina.
—MARTINA NAVRATILOVA,
  Martina Navratilova—Being Myself, 1985

What is new is not bisexuality, but rather the widening of our awareness and acceptance of human capacities for sexual love.
—MARGARET MEAD,
  Redbook, 1975

(See also *Homosexuality, Lesbians*)

Blind Love

Blind love mistakes a harelip for a dimple.
  ➥ Old French proverb

It is not love, but lack of love, that is blind.
  ➥ Glenway Wescott,
     New York Herald Tribune, December 19, 1965

(See also *Falling in Love, First Love, Foolish Love, Forbidden Love, Free Love, Love, Loving, Memories of Love, Unrequited Love, Young Love*)

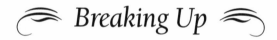

Breaking Up

Why is it that we don't always recognize the moment when love begins but we always know when it ends?
  ➥ Harris K. Telemacher
     in *L.A. Story,* by Steve Martin, 1991

In a separation it is the one who is not really in love who says the more tender things.
  ➥ Marcel Proust,
     Remembrance of Things Past, 1922–1931

I loved you; and perhaps I love you still,
The flame, perhaps, is not extinguished; yet
It burns so quietly within my soul,
No longer should you feel distressed by it.
  ➥ Alexander Pushkin,
     "I Loved You," 1829

It is seldom indeed that one parts on good terms, because if one were on good terms, one would not part.

➤ MARCEL PROUST,
Remembrance of Things Past, 1922–1931

Two separate, distinct personalities, not separate at all, but inextricably bound, soul and body and mind, to each other, how did we get so far apart so fast?

➤ JUDITH GUEST,
Ordinary People, 1976

Then fly betimes, for only they
Conquer Love that run away.

➤ THOMAS CAREW,
"**Conquest by Flight**," 1640

Love frequently dies of time alone—much more frequently of displacement.

➤ THOMAS HARDY,
A Pair of Blue Eyes, 1873

'Tis better to have loved and lost than never to have loved at all.

➤ SAMUEL BUTLER,
The Way of All Flesh, 1903

And I shall find some girl perhaps,
And a better one than you,
With eyes as wise, but kindlier,
And lips as soft, but true,
And I daresay she will do.

➤ RUPERT BROOKE,
"**The Chilterns**," *Complete Poems*, 1992

I hated her now with a hatred more fatal than indifference because it was the other side of love.

➤ AUGUST STRINDBERG,
A Madman's Defence, 1968

When love grows diseased, the best thing we can do is put it to a violent death; I cannot endure the torture of a lingering and consumptive passion.

━━GEORGE ETHEREGE,
The Man of Mode, 1676

And I would have, now love is over,
An end to all, an end:
I cannot, having been your lover,
Stoop to become your friend!

━━ARTHUR SYMONS,
"After Love," 1892

Take me or leave me, or, as is the usual order of things, both.

━━DOROTHY PARKER,
"A Good Novel, and a Great Story," *The New Yorker*, 1928

Love, for both of them, had ceased to be a journey, an adventure, an essay of hope. It had become an infection, a ritual, a drama with a bloody last act, and they could both foresee the final carnage.

━━MARGARET DRABBLE,
The Middle Ground, 1980

(See also *Betrayal, Divorce*)

Brothers

A girl who has a brother has a great advantage over one who hasn't; she gets a working knowledge of men without having to go through the matrimonial inquisition in order to acquire it.

━━HELEN ROWLAND,
Reflections of a Bachelor Girl, 1903

I loved Ophelia: forty thousand brothers
Could not, with all their quantity of love,
Make up my sum.

➤ WILLIAM SHAKESPEARE,
   Hamlet, 1601

(See also *Family, Sisters*)

Cars

There are a number of mechanical devices which increase sexual arousal, particularly in women. Chief among these is the Mercedes-Benz 380SL convertible.

➤ P. J. O'ROURKE,
   Modern Manners, 1984

Remarkable win today, old boy. Only evidence of adultery we had was a pair of footprints upside down on the dashboard of an Austin Seven parked in Hampstead Garden Suburb.

➤ CLIFFORD MORTIMER and JOHN MORTIMER,
   Clinging to the Wreckage, 1982

When a man opens the car door for his wife, it's either a new car or a new wife.

➤ PRINCE PHILIP, DUKE OF EDINBURGH,
   Today, March 2, 1988

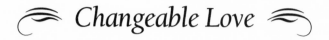 Changeable Love

An inconstant woman, tho' she has no chance to be very happy, can never be very unhappy.

— JOHN GAY,
Polly, 1729

The fickleness of the women I love is only equalled by the infernal constancy of the women who love me.

— GEORGE BERNARD SHAW,
The Philanderer, 1898

Once you admit that you can change the object of a strongly felt affection, you undermine the whole structure of love and marriage, the whole philosophy of Shakespeare's sonnet.

— MURIEL SPARK,
The Girls of Slender Means, 1963

Love is like linen often changed, the sweeter.

— PHINEAS FLETCHER,
Sicelides, 1614

(See also *Blind Love, Enduring Love, Falling in Love, First Love, Foolish Love, Free Love, Love, Loving, Mature Love, Memories of Love, True Love, Young Love*)

 *Charm*

Falling out of love is chiefly a matter of forgetting how charming someone is.

➤ IRIS MURDOCH,
   A Severed Head, 1961

Charm...it's a sort of bloom on a woman. If you have it, you don't need to have anything else; and if you don't have it, it doesn't much matter what else you have.

➤ J. M. BARRIE,
   What Every Woman Knows, 1918

Oozing charm from every pore,
He oiled his way around the floor

➤ ALAN JAY LERNER,
   "You Did It," *My Fair Lady*, 1956

(See also *Attraction, Beauty*)

 *Chastity*

I'm as pure as the driven slush.

➤ TALLULAH BANKHEAD,
   Saturday Evening Post, April 12, 1947

When women go wrong, men go right after them.

➤ MAE WEST,
   She Done Him Wrong, 1933

Most good women are hidden treasures who are only safe because nobody looks for them.

—DOROTHY PARKER,
The New York Times, June 8, 1967

I'll wager you that in 10 years it will be fashionable again to be a virgin.

—BARBARA CARTLAND,
Observer, June 20, 1976

Change in a trice
The lilies and languor of virtue
For the raptures and roses of vice.

—ALGERNON CHARLES SWINBURNE,
"Dolores," 1866

Feminine virtue is nothing but a convenient masculine invention.

—NINON DE LENCLOS,
Letters, 1870

What is it that constitutes virtue, Mrs Graham? Is it the circumstance of being able and willing to resist temptation; or that of having no temptation to resist?

—ANNE BRONTË,
The Tenant of Wildfell Hall, 1848

A woman's chastity consists, like an onion, of a series of coats.

—NATHANIEL HAWTHORNE,
diary, March 16, 1854

(See also *Faithfulness*)

 *Christianity*

Christianity has done a great deal for love by making a sin of it.

━ANATOLE FRANCE,
    The Garden of Epicurus, 1894

(See also *God, Religion*)

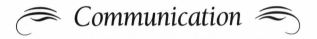 *Communication*

If your husband ceases to call you "Sugarfoot" or "Candy Eyes" or "Cutie Fudge Pie" during the first year of your marriage, it is not necessarily a sign that he has come to take you for granted or that he no longer cares.

━JAMES THURBER,
    Thurber Country, 1953

Spoken love will palliate even spoken roughness. Had he once called her his own Lizzie, he might have scolded her as he pleased.

━ANTHONY TROLLOPE,
    The Eustace Diamonds, 1873

Compatibility

I believe a little incompatibility is the spice of life,
particularly if he has income and she is pattable.
>　—OGDEN NASH,
>　　*I Do, I Will, I Have*, 1949

To be together is for us to be at once as free as in solitude, as gay as
in company. We talk, I believe, all day long; to talk to each other is
but a more animated and an audible thinking.
>　—CHARLOTTE BRONTË,
>　　*Jane Eyre*, 1847

Those who have never known the deep intimacy and the intense
companionship of happy mutual love and missed the best thing
that life has to give; unconsciously, if not consciously, they feel this,
and the resulting disappointment inclines them towards envy,
oppression, and cruelty.
>　—BERTRAND RUSSELL,
>　　*Marriage and Morals*, 1929

Contentment

And what do all the great words come to in the end, but that?—I
love you—I am at rest with you—I have come home.
>　—DOROTHY L. SAYERS,
>　　*Busman's Honeymoon*, 1937

(See also *Happiness*)

Cooking

There is no spectacle on earth more appealing than that of a beautiful woman in the act of cooking dinner for someone she loves.

——THOMAS WOLFE,
The Web and the Rock, 1939

Cooking is like love. It should be entered into with abandon or not at all.

——HARRIET VAN HORNE,
Vogue, October 15, 1956

Kissing don't last; cookery do!

——GEORGE MEREDITH,
The Ordeal of Richard Feverel, 1859

(See also *Food, Wine*)

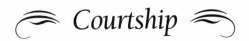

Courtship

Courtship to marriage, as a very witty prologue to a very dull play.

——WILLIAM CONGREVE,
The Old Bachelor, 1693

She knew how to allure by denying, and to make the gift rich by delaying it.

——ANTHONY TROLLOPE,
Phineas Finn, 1869

She'll throw herself at his head until he loses consciousness, and then she'll marry him.

—RUTH SAWYER,
The Primrose Ring, 1915

Come, woo me, woo me; for now I am in a holiday humour, and like enough to consent.

—WILLIAM SHAKESPEARE,
As You Like It, 1599

I've got a heart like a college prom. Each one I dance with seems the best of all.

—ILKA CHASE,
In Bed We Cry, 1943

If you want to win her hand,
Let the maiden understand
That she's not the only pebble on the beach.

—HARRY BRAISTED,
"You're Not the Only Pebble on the Beach," 1896

When someone asks, "Why do you think he's not calling me?" there's always one answer—"He's not interested." There's not ever any other answer.

—FRAN LEBOWITZ,
Mirabella, 1992

Wooing, so tiring.

—NANCY MITFORD,
The Pursuit of Love, 1945

We have progressively improved into a less spiritual species of tenderness—but the seal is not yet fixed though the wax is preparing for the impression.

—LORD BYRON,
of his relationship with Lady Frances Webster,
letter to Lady Melbourne, October 14, 1813

Make love to every woman you meet. If you get five percent on your outlays, it's a good investment.

—ARNOLD BENNETT,
    quoted in *Quotations for Our Time* by Laurence J. Peter, ed.,
    1977

There is too little courtship in the world... For courtship means a wish to stand well in the other person's eyes, and what is more, a readiness to be pleased with the other's ways; a sense on each side of having had the better of the bargain; an undercurrent of surprise and thankfulness at one's good luck.

—VERNON LEE,
    "In Praise of Courtship," *Hortus Vitae*, 1904

If I am not worth the wooing, I surely am not worth the winning.

—HENRY WADSWORTH LONGFELLOW,
    The Courtship of Miles Standish, 1858

Everyone knows that dating in your thirties is not the happy-go-lucky free-for-all it was when you were twenty-two.

—HELEN FIELDING,
    Bridget Jones' Diary, 1996

There are very few of us who have heart enough to be really in love without encouragement. In nine cases out of ten, a woman had better show more affection than she feels.

—JANE AUSTEN,
    Pride and Prejudice, 1813

Man is the hunter, woman is his game:
The sleek and shining creatures of the chase,
We hunt them for the beauty of their skins;
They love us for it; and we ride them down.

—ALFRED, LORD TENNYSON,
    "The Princess," 1847

Ten years of courtship is carrying celibacy to extremes.

    ◆—ALAN BENNETT,
       Habeas Corpus, 1973

It's amazing how much time and money can be saved in the world of dating by close attention to detail. A white sock here, a pair of red braces there, a grey slip-on shoe, a swastika, are as often as not all one needs to tell you there's no point in writing down phone numbers and forking out for expensive lunches because it's never going to be a runner.

    ◆—HELEN FIELDING,
       Bridget Jones' Diary, 1996

We've got to have
We plot to have
For it's so dreary not to have
That certain thing called the Boy Friend

    ◆—SANDY WILSON,
       "The Boyfriend," 1954

You think that you are Ann's suitor; that you are the pursuer and she the pursued... Fool: it is you who are the pursued, the marked down quarry, the destined prey.

    ◆—GEORGE BERNARD SHAW,
       Man and Superman, 1903

 *Dancing*

Everybody knows that the real business of a ball is either to look out for a wife, to look after a wife, or to look after somebody else's wife.

    ◆—R. S. SURTEES,
       Mr. Facey Romford's Hounds, 1865

Dancing is a wonderful training for girls, it's the first way you learn to guess what a man is going to do before he does it.

➤ CHRISTOPHER MORLEY,
Kitty Foyle, 1939

Dancing begets warmth, which is the parent of wantonness. It is, Sir, the great grandfather of cuckoldom.

➤ HENRY FIELDING,
Love in Several Masques, 1728

Dancing is a perpendicular expression of a horizontal desire.

➤ GEORGE BERNARD SHAW,
New Statesman, March 23, 1962

I've got a heart like a college prom. Each one I dance with seems the best of all.

➤ ILKA CHASE,
In Bed We Cry, 1943

This wondrous miracle did Love devise,
for dancing is love's proper exercise

➤ JOHN DAVIES,
"Orchestra, or a Poem of Dancing," 1596

 *Death*

... as they die, the ones we love, we lose our witnesses, our watchers, those who know and understand the tiny little meaningless patterns, those words drawn in water with a stick. And there is nothing left but the endless flow.

➤ ANNE RICE,
The Witching Hour, 1990

Mine eyes wax heavy and ye day grows old.
The dew falls thick, my beloved grows cold.
Draw, draw ye closed curtains and make room:
My dear, my dearest dust; I come, I come.

    ➤CATHERINE DYER,
        epitaph on the monument of Sir William Dyer at Colmworth,
        1641

Love made me poet,
And this I writ;
My heart did do it,
and not my wit.

    ➤ELIZABETH, LADY TANFIELD,
        epitaph for her husband in Burford Parish Church, Oxford-
        shire

Love is the only effective counter to death.

    ➤MAUREEN DUFFY,
        Wounds, 1969

He was comforted by one of the simpler emotions which some
human beings are lucky enough to experience. He knew when he
died, he would be watched by someone he loved.

    ➤NOEL ANNAN,
        on E. M. Forster,
        London Observer, March 11, 1979

Every arrival foretells a leave-taking; every birth a death. Yet each
death and departure comes to us as a surprise, a sorrow never
anticipated.

    ➤JESSAMYN WEST,
        The Life I Really Lived, 1979

Many who spent a lifetime in it can tell us less of love than the
child who lost a dog yesterday.

    ➤THORNTON WILDER,
        quoted in *The American Scholar Reader* by Hiran Hayden and
        Betsy Saunders, eds., 1960

For my Embalming (Sweetest) there will be
No Spices wanting, when I'm laid by thee.

    ROBERT HERRICK,
      "To Anthea: Now Is the Time," 1648

She is far from the land where her young hero sleeps,
And lovers are round her, sighing:
But coldly she turns from their gaze, and weeps,
For her heart in his grave is lying.

    THOMAS MOORE,
      "She Is Far," *Irish Melodies,*1834

I have two luxuries to brood over in my walks, your loveliness and the
hour of my death. O that I could have possession of them both in the
same minute.

    JOHN KEATS,
      letter to Fanny Brawne, July 25, 1819

Longing for that lovely lady
How can I bring my aching heart to rest?

    HAN WU-TI,
      on the death of his mistress, 157–87 B.C.

Let's contend no more, Love,
Strive nor weep:
All be as before, Love,
—Only sleep!

    ROBERT BROWNING,
      "A Woman's Last Word," 1855

I love thee with a love I seemed to lose
With my lost saints—I love thee with the breath,
Smiles, tears, of all my life!—and, if God choose,
I shall but love thee better after death.

    ELIZABETH BARRETT BROWNING,
      Sonnets from the Portuguese, 1850

The grave's a fine and private place,
But none, I think, do there embrace.
　　━ANDREW MULDOON,
　　　　"Incantata," 1994

When I am dead and over me bright April
Shakes out her rain-drenched hair,
Though you should lean above me
Broken-hearted,
I shall not care.
　　━SARA TEASDALE,
　　　　"I Shall Not Care," 1919

How alike the groans of love to those of the dying.
　　━MALCOLM LOWRY,
　　　　Under the Volcano, 1947

 *Delicacy*

Delicacy is to love what grace is to beauty.
　　━FRANÇOISE D'AUBIGNE DE MAINTENON,
　　　　quoted in *Uncommon Scold* by Abby Adams, 1989

 *Desire*

How helpless we are, like netted birds, when we are caught by
desire!
　　━BELVA PLAIN,
　　　　Evergreen, 1978

Is it not strange that desire should so many years outlive perform-
ance?

    ⬅ WILLIAM SHAKESPEARE,
      Henry IV, Part 2, 1597

It is human nature to overestimate the thing you've never had.

    ⬅ ELLEN GLASGOW,
      The Romantic Comedians, 1926

The absolute yearning of one human body for another particular
one and its indifference to substitutes is one of life's major mys-
teries.

    ⬅ IRIS MURDOCH,
      The Black Prince, 1973

The desire of the moth for the star,
Of the night for the morrow,
The devotion to something afar
From the sphere of our sorrow.

    ⬅ PERCY BYSSHE SHELLEY,
      "One Word Is Too Often Profaned," 1824

Only I discern—
Infinite passing, and the pain
Of finite hearts that yearn.

    ⬅ ROBERT BROWNING,
      Two in the Campagna, 1855

She went on gazing at Leonidas with the expression of a six year
old contemplating a large slice of chocolate cake.

    ⬅ SARAH CAUDWELL,
      The Shortest Way to Hades, 1984

There is nothing like desire for preventing the things one says from
bearing any resemblance to what one has in one's mind.

    ⬅ MARCEL PROUST,
      The Guermantes Way, 1921

You can have anything you want if you want it desperately enough. You must want it with an inner exuberance that erupts through the skin and joins the energy that created the world.

—SHEILAH GRAHAM,
The Rest of the Story, 1964

(See also *Seduction*)

Dieting

Give me a dozen heartbreaks if you think it would help me lose one pound.

—COLETTE,
Cheri, 1920

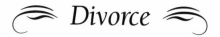

Divorce

Divorce is like an amputation. You survive, but there is less of you.

—MARGARET ATWOOD,
Time, 1973

There is a rhythm to the ending of a marriage just like the rhythm of a courtship—only backward. You try to start again but get into blaming over and over. Finally you are both worn out, exhausted, hopeless. Then the lawyers are called in to pick clean the corpses. The death has occurred much earlier.

—ERICA JONG,
How to Save Your Own Life, 1977

Being divorced is like being hit by a Mack truck. If you live through it, you start looking very carefully to the right and to the left.
— JEAN KERR,
   Mary, Mary, 1963

Reports of a divorce are totally false. There are no plans, nor have there been, for divorce. After 30 years, we now own 18,352 things: had there ever been plans for divorce, Europe would have spotted tea-chests stretching round the block.
— ALAN COREN,
   A Bit on the Side, 1995

I doubt if there is one married person on earth who can be objective about divorce. It is always a threat, admittedly or not, and such a dire threat that it is almost a dirty word.
— NORA JOHNSON,
   Atlantic, July 1962

So many people think divorce a panacea for every ill, who find out, when they try it, the remedy is worse than the disease.
— DOROTHY DIX,
   Dorothy Dix, Her Book, 1926

However often marriage is dissolved, it remains indissoluble. Real divorce, the divorce of heart and nerve and fiber, does not exist, since there is no divorce from memory.
— VIRGINIA PETERSON,
   A Matter of Life and Death, 1961

Divorce is only less painful than the need for divorce.
— JANE O'REILLY,
   The Girl I Left Behind, 1980

When a marriage ends, who is left to understand it?
— JOYCE CAROL OATES,
   The Wheel of Love and Other Stories, 1970

Could you possibly have settled down to the old life and forgotten the fairy land through when you had passed? My child, I do not think so.

> ➤ ERNEST SIMPSON,
> in a 1936 letter to his estranged wife Wallis Warfield Simpson, after Edward VIII's abdication

(See also *Betrayal, Breaking Up*)

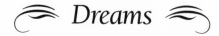

Dreams

If I had never met him I would have dreamed him into being.

> ➤ ANZIA YERIERSKA,
> *Red Ribbon on a White Horse*, 1950

Dreaming is the poor retreat of the lazy, hopeless and imperfect lover.

> ➤ WILLIAM CONGREVE,
> *Love for Love*, 1695

(See also *Sleep*)

Emotions

A belief which does not spring from a conviction of the emotions is no belief at all.

> ➤ EVELYN SCOTT,
> *Escapade*, 1923

No emotion is the final one.

—JEANETTE WINTERSON,
Oranges Are Not the Only Fruit, 1985

If you haven't had at least a slight poetic crack in the heart, you have been cheated by nature.

—PHYLLIS BATTELLE,
New York Journal-American, June 1, 1962

Those who don't know how to weep with their whole heart don't know how to laugh, either.

—GOLDA MEIR,
in an interview in *Ms magazine*, 1973

To have felt too much is to end in feeling nothing.

—DOROTHY THOMPSON,
on waiting in the courthouse for divorce from Sinclair Lewis,
quoted in *Dorothy and Red* by Vincent Sheen, 1963

You have too many feelings, but not nearly enough love.

—EVELYN UNDERHILL,
quoted in *The Letters of Evelyn Underhill* by Charles Williams,
ed., 1943

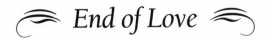

End of Love

After all, my erstwhile dear
My no longer cherished
Need we say it was not there
Just because it perished?

—EDNA ST. VINCENT MILLAY,
"Passer Mortuus Est," *Second April*, 1921

Love never dies of starvation, but often of indigestion.

➤NINON DE LENCLOS,
L'Esprit des Autres

When love turns away, now, I don't follow it. I sit and suffer, unprotesting, until I feel the tread of another step.

➤SYLVIA ASHTON-WARNER,
Teacher, 1963

Love never dies quite suddenly. He complains a great deal before expiring.

➤MINNA THOMAS ANTRIM,
Sweathearts and Beaux, 1905

How do you know that love is gone? If you said you would be there at seven, you get there by nine and he or she has not called the police yet—it's gone.

➤MARLENE DIETRICH,
Marlene Dietrich's ABC, 1962

(See also *Betrayal, Divorce, Forbidden Love, Heartbreak, Love vs. Hate, Memories of Love, Parting, Unrequited Love*)

Enduring Love

I'll love you, dear, I'll love you
Till China and Africa meet
And the river jumps over the mountain
And the salmon sing in the street.

➤W. H. AUDEN,
"As I Walked Out One Evening," 1940

Many waters cannot quench love, neither can the floods drown it.
➤ Song of Solomon 8:7

And o'er the hills and far away
Beyond their utmost purple rim,
Beyond the night, across the day,
Through all the world she followed him.
➤ ALFRED, LORD TENNYSON,
"The Day Dream," 1842

Lie to me. Tell me that all these years you've waited. Tell me.
➤ PHILIP YORDAN,
Johnny Guitar, 1954

Sometimes idiosyncrasies which used to be irritating become endearing, part of the complexity of a partner who has become woven deep into our own selves.
➤ MADELEINE L'ENGLE,
Two-Part Invention, 1988

Even when the first wild desire is gone, especially then, there is an inherent need for good manners and consideration, for the putting forth of effort. Two courteous and civilized human beings out of the loneliness of their souls owe that to each other.
➤ ILKA CHASE,
In Bed We Cry, 1943

When we are not in love too much, we are not in love enough.
➤ COMTE DE BUSSY-RABUTIN,
Histoire Amoureuse des Gaules: Maximes d' Amour, 1665

"Nothing, so it seems to me," said the stranger, "is more beautiful than the love that has weathered the storms of life... The love of the young for the young, that is the beginning of life. But the love of the old for the old, that is the beginning of—of things longer."
➤ JEROME K. JEROME,
The Passing of the Third Floor Back, 1908

She cannot fade, though thou hast not thy bliss,
For ever wilt thou love and she be fair.
    —JOHN KEATS,
      Ode on a Grecian Urn, 1820

As fair art thou, my bonie lass,
So deep in luve am I,
And I will luve thee still, my dear,
Till a' the seas gang dry.
    —ROBERT BURNS,
      "My Luve Is Like a Red Red Rose" (derived from folksongs),
      1796

Escape me?
Never—
Beloved!
While I am I, and you are you.
    —ROBERT BROWNING,
      "Life in a Love," 1855

None shall part us from each other,
One in life and death are we:
All in all to one another—
I to thee and thou to me!
    —SIR WILLIAM S. GILBERT,
      Iolanthe, 1882

My bounty is as boundless as the sea,
My love as deep; the more I give to thee,
The more I have, for both are infinite.
    —WILLIAM SHAKESPEARE,
      Romeo and Julliet, 1595

True love isn't the kind that endures through long years of absence,
but the kind that endures through long years of propinquity.
    —HELEN ROWLAND,
      A Guide to Men, 1922

As you are woman, so be lovely;
As you are lovely, so be various;
Merciful as constant, constant as various,
So be mine, as I your for ever.

    ━Robert Von Ranke Graves,
       Pygmalion to Galatea

The struggle is over and I have found peace. I think today I could let you marry another without losing it—for I know the spiritual union between us will outlive this life, even if we never see each other in this world again.

    ━Maud Gonne,
       letter to W. B. Yeats, December 1908

Let me not to the marriage of true minds
Admit impediments. Love is not love
Which alters when it alteration finds,
Or bends with the remover to remove:
O, no! It is an ever-fixed mark,
That looks on tempests and is never shaken.

    ━William Shakespeare,
       Sonnet 116

(See also *Falling in Love, First Love, Love at First Sight, Loving, Mature Love, Memories of Love, True Love*)

 *Engagement*

I am to be married within three days; married past redemption.

    ━John Dryden,
       Marriage à la Mode, 1672

An engaged woman is always more agreeable than a disengaged. She is satisfied with herself, her cares are over, and she feels that she may exert all her powers of pleasing without suspicion.
➤ JANE AUSTEN,
Mansfield Park,1814

Of all the stages in a woman's life, none is so dangerous as the period between her acknowledgment of a passion for a man, and the day set apart for her nuptials.
➤ HUGH KELLY,
Memoirs of a Magdalen, 1767

Look, how my ring encompasseth thy finger,
Even so thy breast encloseth my poor heart;
Wear both of them, for both of them are thine.
➤ WILLIAM SHAKESPEARE,
Venus and Adonis, 1593

Surely the whole point of an engagement is the ring! It's a get-out clause with accompanying jewelry.
➤ JEAN BUCHANAN,
The Wild House, 1998 BBC series

We will have rings, and things, and fine array;
And kiss me Kate, we will be married o' Sunday.
➤ WILLIAM SHAKESPEARE,
The Taming of the Shrew, 1592

Opportunity knocks for every man, but you have to give a woman a ring.
➤ MAE WEST,
quoted in *Peel Me a Grape* by Joseph Weintraub, 1975

(See also *Marriage*)

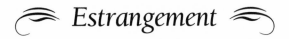

Estrangement

There was no passion in her feeling for him, and no relief from its daily pressure. It was like being loved by a large, moist sponge.

➤ PHYLLIS BOTTOME,
   "The Other Island," *Strange Fruit*, 1928

Sleep on, I sit and watch your tent in silence
White as a sail upon this sandy sea,
And know the Desert' self is not more boundless
Than is the distance 'twixt yourself and me

➤ LAURENCE HOPE,
   "Stars of the Desert," 1903

(See also *Betrayal, Breaking Up, Divorce*)

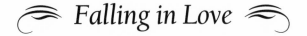

Falling in Love

If it is your time love will track you down like a cruise missile. If you say "No! I don't want it right now," that's when you'll get it for sure.

➤ LYNDA BARRY,
   Big Ideas, 1983

Love can find an entrance, not only into an open heart, but also into a heart well fortified, if watch be not well kept.

➤ FRANCIS BACON,
   Essays, 1625

Falling in love is not an extension of one's limits or boundaries, it is a partial and temporary collapse of them.

➤ M. SCOTT PECK,
The Road Less Travelled, 1978

Many a man has fallen in love with a girl in a light so dim he would not have chosen a suit by it.

➤ MAURICE CHEVALIER,
News Summaries, July 17, 1955

He would have fallen in love with me, I think, if I had been built like Brunhilde and had a mustache and the mind of an Easter chick.

➤ ANNE RIVERS SIDDONS,
Hill Towns, 1993

When first we fall in love, we feel that we know all there is to know about life. And perhaps we are right.

➤ MIGNON MCLAUGHLIN,
The Neurotic's Notebook, 1963

Falling in love consists merely in uncorking the imagination and bottling the common sense.

➤ HELEN ROWLAND,
A Guide to Men, 1922

To fall in love you have to be in the state of mind for it to take, like a disease.

➤ NANCY MITFORD,
quoted in *Uncommon Scold* by Abby Adams, 1989

I cannot fix on the hour, or the spot, or the look, or the words, which laid the foundation. It is too long ago. I was in the middle before I knew I had begun.

➤ JANE AUSTEN,
Pride and Prejudice, 1813

Oh, what a dear ravishing thing is the beginning of an Amour!

──APHRA BEHN,
The Emperor of the Moon, 1687

(See also *Blind Love, Changeable Love, First Love, Foolish Love, Forbidden Love, Free Love, Love, Love at First Sight, Loving, Mature Love, Memories of Love, True Love, Unrequited Love, Young Love*)

Faithfulness

I have been faithful to thee, Cynara! In my fashion.

──ERNEST DOWSON,
Non Sum Qualis Eram, 1896

Entreat me not to leave thee, or to return from following after thee; for whither thou goest, I will go; and where thou lodgest, I will lodge; thy people shall be my people, and thy God, my God. Where thou diest, will I die, and there will I be buried: the Lord do so to me, and more also, if aught but death part thee and me.

──The Book of Ruth 1:16-17

And when, throughout all the wild orgasms of love
slowly a gem forms, in the ancient, once-more-molten rocks
of two human hearts, two ancient rocks, a man's heart and a
    woman's,
that is the crystal of peace, the slow hard jewel of trust,
the sapphire of fidelity.

──D. H. LAWRENCE,
"Fidelity," from *Pansies*, 1928

Will he always love me?
I cannot read his heart.
This morning my thoughts
Are as disordered
As my black hair.
—HORIKAWA,
One Hundred Poems from the Japanese, 1964

The highest level of sexual excitement is in a monogamous relationship.
—WARREN BEATTY,
Observer, October 27, 1991

There is always something left to love. And if you haven't learned that, you ain't learned nothing.
—LORRAINE HANSBERRY,
A Raisin in the Sun, 1959

My true love hath my heart and I have his,
By just exchange one for the other giv'n;
I hold his dear, and mine he cannot miss,
There never was a better bargain driv'n.
—PHILIP SIDNEY,
"Arcadia, 1581

Constancy...the small change of love, which people exact so rigidly, receive in such counterfeit coin, and repay in baser metal.
—LORD BYRON,
letter to Thomas Moore, November 17, 1816

No, the heart that has truly loved never forgets,
But as truly loves on to the close,
As the sunflower turns on her god, when he sets,
The same look which she turned when he rose.
—THOMAS MOORE,
"Believe Me, If All Those Endearing Young Charms," 1807

My dear and only love, I pray
This noble world of thee,
Be governed by no other sway
But purest monarchy.
For if confusion have a part,
Which virtuous souls abhor,
And hold a synod in thy heart,
I'll never love thee more.

> —JAMES GRAHAM,
> Marquess of Montrose,
> *My Dear and Only Love*, ca 1642

Those who are faithless know the pleasures of love; it is the faithful
who know love's tragedies.

> —OSCAR WILDE,
> *The Picture of Dorian Gray*, 1891

To Sorrow I bade good-morrow,
And thought to leave her far away behind;
But cheerly, cheerly,
She loves me dearly;
She is so constant to me, and so kind.

> —JOHN KEATS,
> *Endymion*, 1818

The fickleness of the women I love is only equalled by the infernal
constancy of the women who love me.

> —GEORGE BERNARD SHAW,
> *The Philanderer*, 1893

I would not leave you in times of trouble
We never could have come this far
I took the good times, I'll take the bad times
I'll take you just the way you are.

> —BILLY JOEL,
> "Just the Way You Are," 1977

We only part to meet again.
Change, as ye list, ye winds; my heart shall be
The faithful compass that still points to thee.

  ✎ JOHN GAY,
    "Sweet William's Farewell to Black-Eyed Susan," 1720

(See also *Enduring Love, Famous Lovers, First Love, Foolish Love, Forbidden Love, Free Love, Love, Love at First Sight, Loving, Mature Love, Memories of Love, True Love, Young Love*)

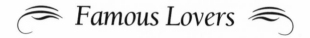

Famous Lovers

Twenty-nine years! It seems like twenty-nine days. Detroit, Port Huron, a shirt store, County Judge, defeat, Margie, Automobile Club membership drive, Presiding Judge, Senator, V. P., now! You still are on the pedestal where I placed you that day in Sunday school in 1890. What an old fool I am.

  ✎ HARRY S TRUMAN,
    letter to his wife, Bess, on their wedding anniversary, June 24,
      1948

I might run from her for a thousand years and she is still my baby child…. Our love is so furious that we burn each other out.

  ✎ RICHARD BURTON,
    after his second divorce from Elizabeth Taylor,
    recalled on his death, August 5, 1984

In my Sunday school class there was a beautiful little girl with golden curls. I was smitten at once and still am.

  ✎ HARRY S TRUMAN,
    on his wife, Bess,
    news summaries, December 31, 1952

I've had the boyhood thing of being Elvis. Now I want to be with my best friend, and my best friend's my wife. Who could ask for anything more?

➤ JOHN LENNON,
interview on RKO Radio New York, December 8, 1980

I never see a flower that pleases me, but I wish for you.

➤ WILLIAM WORDSWORTH,
letter to his wife, 1810

He spoke of love and the Supreme Court.

➤ ELIZABETH BLACK,
on marriage proposal from Supreme Court Justice Hugo L.
Black,
Christian Science Monitor, February 27, 1986

So you wound up with Apollo
If he's sometimes hard to swallow
Use this.

➤ PAUL NEWMAN,
inscription on silver sherry cup given to his wife Joanne
Woodward,
The New York Times, September 28, 1986

I feel the loss more than I had thought I should.... Without my wishing it she chose to lose herself in me, and the result was she became truly my better half.

➤ MAHATMA GANDHI,
on the death of his wife Kasturba,
in Arun Gandhi, *Daughter of Midnight: The Child Bride of
Gandhi*, 1998

It is not in my power to tell thee how I have been affected by this dearest of all letters—it was so unexpected—so new a thing to see the breathing of the inmost heart upon paper.

➤ MARY WORDSWORTH,
letter to William Wordsworth, August 1, 1810

It was with some emotion…that I beheld Albert—who is beautiful.

> ━━QUEEN VICTORIA,
> of her first meeting with Prince Albert (ca 1838),
> attributed in *Albert: Uncrowned King* by Stanley Weintraub,
> 1997

First I lost weight, then I lost my voice, and now I've lost Onassis.

> ━━MARIA CALLAS,
> quoted in *Woman's Almanac* by Barbara McDowell and Hana
> Umlauf, 1977

Everywhere we go, Nancy makes the world a little better.

> ━━RONALD REAGAN,
> on his wife in film at Republican National Convention,
> August 22, 1984

You're beautiful, like a May fly.

> ━━ERNEST HEMINGWAY,
> to his future wife Mary,
> recalled on her death, November 26, 1986

Charles is life itself—pure life, force, like sunlight—and it is for this that I married him and this that holds me to him, caring always, caring desperately what happens to him and whatever he happens to be involved in.

> ━━ANNE MORROW LINDBERGH,
> *War Within and Without*, 1980

The love we have in our youth is superficial compared to the love that an old man has for his old wife.

> ━━WILL DURANT,
> on his 90th birthday,
> *The New York Times*, November 6, 1975

I am marrying her because I love her.

> ━━CROWN PRINCE AKIHITO of Japan,
> on becoming first member of Japanese royal family to wed a
> commoner,
> news summaries, April 12, 1959

When the winds blow and the rains fall and the sun shines through the clouds...he still resolves as he did then, that nothing so fine ever happened to him or anyone else as falling in love with Thee— my dearest heart.

> ―RICHARD M. NIXON,
> letter to his future wife Pat,
> quoted in *Pat Nixon* by Julie Nixon Eisenhower, 1986

Two such as you with such a master speed
Cannot be parted nor be swept away
From one another once you are agreed
That life is only life forevermore
Together wing to wing and oar to oar.

> ―ROBERT FROST,
> inscribed on gravestone of Frost and his wife Elinor

It took great courage to ask a beautiful young woman to marry me. Believe me, it is easier to play the whole of Petruska on the piano.

> ―ARTUR RUBINSTEIN,
> *A Little Night Music*, 1964

I was shocked and angry...with the startling suggestion that I should send from my land, my realm, the woman I intended to marry.

> ―EDWARD, DUKE OF WINDSOR,
> recalling political advice to send Wallis Warfield Simpson
> abroad without further delay,
> *A King's Story*, 1951

P.S. It's all gossip about the prince. I'm not in the habit of taking my girlfriend's beaux.

> ―WALLIS WARFIELD SIMPSON, DUCHESS OF WINDSOR,
> letter to her aunt, February 18, 1934

"Mad, bad, and dangerous to know."

> ―LADY CAROLINE LAMB,
> of Lord Byron,
> diary, March 1812

Lyndon was the most outspoken, straightforward, determined person I'd ever encountered. I knew I'd met something remarkable—but I didn't know quite what.

> ⊸CLAUDIA "LADY BIRD" JOHNSON,
> on meeting her future husband,
> *Saturday Evening Post*, February 8, 1964

It was an unspoken pleasure, that having come together so many years, ruined so much and repaired a little, we had endured.

> ⊸LILLIAN HELLMAN,
> on her relationship with Dashiell Hammett,
> recalled on her death on June 30, 1984

We've got this gift of love, but love is like a precious plant. You can't just accept it and leave it in the cupboard or just think it's going to get on by itself. You've got to keep watering it; really look after it and nurture it.

> ⊸JOHN LENNON,
> *Man of the Decade*, broadcast, December 30, 1969

It was a very spasmodic courtship, conducted mainly at long distance with a great clanking of coins in dozens of phone booths.

> ⊸JACQUELINE KENNEDY ONASSIS,
> on her romance with John F. Kennedy,
> quoted in *The Fitzgeralds and the Kennedys* by Doris Kearns Goodwin, 1987

Number 4 should have been number 1. Thanks, Honey.

> ⊸JACK DEMPSEY,
> dedicating his autobiography to his fourth wife,
> in "Unforgettable Jack Dempsey," *Readers Digest*, November 1985

When he's late for dinner, I know he's either having an affair or is lying dead in the street. I always hope it's the street.

> ⊸JESSICA TANDY,
> on her husband Hume Cronyn,
> Kennedy Center Honors, CBS-TV, December 26, 1986

One reason we lasted so long is that we usually played two people who were very much in love. As we were realistic actors, we became those two people. So we had a divertissement: I had an affair with him, and he with me.

> ⟵LYNN FONTANNE,
> on being married for 55 years to costar Alfred Lunt,
> *The New York Times*, April 24, 1978

If I were young and handsome as I was, instead of old and faded as I am, and you could lay the empire of the world at my feet, you should never share the heart and hand that once belonged to John, Duke of Marlborough.

> ⟵SARAH, DUCHESS OF MARLBOROUGH,
> refusing an offer of marriage from the Duke of Somerset,
> quoted in *Marlborough: His Life and Times* by W. S. Churchill,
> vol. 4, 1938

My heart's just a mush this evening. I'm consumed by passion for you and it couldn't be more painful. This has been brewing all day and it came down on me like a tornado in the streets of Douarnenex, where I broke into sobs.

> ⟵SIMONE DE BEAUVOIR,
> letter to Jean-Paul Sartre, September 25, 1939

I didn't wind up in the grotto with a bunch of Playmates; I wound up in bed with my wife and children at 10:30 P.M. watching Murder One. What people don't understand about me is that there is no dark side to my life.

> ⟵HUGH HEFNER,
> on his 70th birthday celebration,
> *Guardian*, April 25, 1996

Here I am back and still smouldering with passion, like wine smoking. Not a passion any longer for flesh, but a complete hunger for you, a devouring hunger.

> ⟵HENRY MILLER,
> letter to Anais Nin, August 14, 1932

But if it pleases you to play the part of a true, loyal mistress and friend, and to give yourself body and heart to me, who will be, and has been, your most loyal servant (if your rigour does not forbid me), I promise you that not only will you deserve the name, but also that I will take you for my only mistress, casting all others, that are in competition with you, out of my thoughts and affection, and serving only you.

— HENRY VIII,
letter to Anne Boleyn, 1527

Please fence me in baby the world's too big out here and I don't like it without you.

— HUMPHREY BOGART,
telegram to Lauren Bacall,
quoted in *Lauren Bacall: By Myself* by Lauren Bacall, 1976

I did hate so, to have to take off the ring. You will have to take the trouble of putting in on again, some day.

— ELIZABETH BARRETT BROWNING,
letter to Robert Browning, September 14, 1846

(See also *First Love, Foolish Love, Forbidden Love, Free Love, Love, Love at First Sight, Loving, Mature Love, Memories of Love, True Love, Young Love*)

 *Farewell*

Slow are the steps of those who leave their love behind.
— **Old English proverb**

In all separations there are the elements of eternity, and in every farewell to the being we love, we set foot upon an undug grave.
— MARY ADAMS,
Confessions of a Wife, 1902

(See also *Death, Parting*)

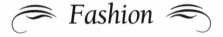 *Fashion*

It's amazing how much time and money can be saved in the world of dating by close attention to detail. A white sock here, a pair of red braces there, a grey slip-on shoe, a swastika, are as often as not all one needs to tell you there's no point writing down phone numbers and forking out for expensive lunches because it's never going to be a runner.
— HELEN FIELDING,
Bridget Jones' Diary, 1996

To teach thee, I am naked first: why then what need'st thou have more covering than a man.
— JOHN DONNE,
"To His Mistress Going to Bed," 1595

When as in silks my Julia goes,
Then, then (methinks) how sweetly flows
That liquefaction of her clothes.
Next, when I cast mine eyes and see
That brave vibration each way free;
O how that glittering taketh me!

> ❧ ROBERT HERRICK,
> "Upon Julia's Clothes," 1648

 *Fear*

Of all forms of caution, caution in love is perhaps the most fatal to true happiness.

> ❧ BERTRAND RUSSELL,
> *The Conquest of Happiness*, 1930

Love, like fire, cannot survive without continual movement, and it ceases to live as soon as it ceases to hope or fear.

> ❧ DUC DE LA ROCHEFOUCAULD,
> *Maximes*, 1678

Faint heart never won fair lady.

> ❧ Proverb

I tremble for what we are doing. Are you sure you will love me for ever? Shall we never repent?

> ❧ LADY MARY WORTLEY MONTAGU,
> letter to Edward Wortley Montagu, August 15, 1712

None but the brave deserves the fair.

> ❧ JOHN DRYDEN,
> *Alexander's Feast*, 1697

For stony limits cannot hold love out,
And what love can do that dares love attempt.

    ━WILLIAM SHAKESPEARE,
      Romeo and Juliet, 1595

 *Feelings*

Better to be without logic than without feeling.

    ━EMILY BRONTË,
      The Professor, 1846

You have too many "feelings," but not nearly enough love.

    ━EVELYN UNDERHILL,
      quoted in *The Letters of Evelyn Underhill* by Charles
      Williams, ed., 1943

You cannot know what you do not feel.

    MARYA MANNERS,
      They, 1968

People who cannot feel punish those who do.

    ━MAY SARTON,
      Mrs. Stevens Hears the Mermaids Singing, 1965

(See also *Desire, Emotions, Passion*)

 *First Love*

The magic of our first love is our ignorance that it can ever end.
➤ BENJAMIN DISRAELI,
Henrietta Temple, 1837

It was first love. There's no love like that. I don't wish it on a soul.
I don't hate anyone enough.
➤ CAROL MATTHAU,
Among the Portuguese, 1992

Deep as first love, and wild with all regret.
➤ ALFRED, LORD TENNYSON,
Songs from *The Princess*, 1850

It was the kind of desperate, headlong, adolescent calf love that he
should have experienced years ago and got over.
➤ AGATHA CHRISTIE,
Remembered Death, 1945

I'm glad it cannot happen twice, the fever of first love.
➤ DAPHNE DU MAURIER,
Rebecca, 1938

Men always want to be a woman's first love. That is their clumsy
vanity. We women have a more subtle instinct about things. What
we like is to be a man's last romance.
➤ OSCAR WILDE, writing in
A Woman of No Importance, 1893

First love is an astounding experience and if the object happens to
be totally unworthy and the love not really love at all, it makes little difference to the intensity or the pain.
➤ ANGELA THIRKELL,
Cheerfulness Breaks In, 1941

I thought that spring must last forevermore
For I was young and loved, and it was May.

—Vera Brittain,
Poems of the War and After, 1934

In her first passion woman loves her lover,
In all the others all she loves is love.

—Lord Byron,
Don Juan, 1819–1824

(See also *Blind Love, Changeable Love, Enduring Love, Falling in
Love, Foolish Love, Forbidden Love, Free Love, Love, Love at First
Sight, Loving, Mature Love, Memories of Love, True Love, Unrequited
Love, Young Love*)

Flowers

Go, lovely rose!
Tell her, that wastes her time and me,
That now she knows,
When I resemble her to thee,
How sweet and fair she seems to be.

—Edmund Waller,
"Go, Lovely Rose!," 1645

The mulish short-sightedness of most Englishmen is such that they
do not give women flowers, because they themselves can see no
point to it—an attitude about as logical as refusing to bait a hook
with a worm because you yourself are no worm-eater.

—Katharine Whitehorn,
Roundabout, 1962

From my experience of life I believe my personal motto should be "Beware of men bearing flowers."
    — MURIEL SPARK,
        Curriculum Vitae, 1992

 *Food*

Chocolate is something you have an affair with.
    — GENEEN ROTH,
        Feeding the Hungry Heart, 1982

[The quince] has the perfume of a loved woman and the same hardness of heart, but it has the colour of the impassioned and scrawny lover.
    — ANONYMOUS,
        Shafer ben Utman-al-Mustafi, ca 950

There is no love sincerer than the love of food.
    — GEORGE BERNARD SHAW,
        Man and Superman, 1903

If you don't love life, you can't enjoy an oyster.
    — ELEANOR CLARK,
        The Oysters of Locmariaquer, 1964

We can only love a person who eats what we eat.
    — RIGOBERTA MENCHU,
        quoted in *I, Rigoberta Menchu* by Elisabeth Burgos-Debray, ed., 1983

(See also *Cooking, Wine*)

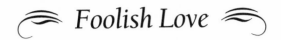 *Foolish Love*

First love is only a little foolishness and a lot of curiosity.

—GEORGE BERNARD SHAW,
John Bull's Other Island, 1907

Love is blind, and lovers cannot see
The pretty follies that themselves commit

—WILLIAM SHAKESPEARE,
The Merchant of Venice, 1596

We love what we would scorn if we were wiser.

—MARIE DE FRANCE,
quoted in *Medieval Fables of Marie de France* by Jeanette Beer,
1981

If thou remember'st not the slightest folly
That ever love did make thee run into,
Thou hast not loved.

—WILLIAM SHAKESPEARE,
As You Like It, 1599

A woman has got to love a bad man once or twice in her life, to be
thankful for a good one.

—MARJORIE KINNAN RAWLINGS,
The Yearling, 1938

I am two fools, I know,
For loving, and for saying so
In whining poetry.

—JOHN DONNE,
"The Triple Fool" in *Poems of John Donne, vol. 1*, E. K. Cham-
bers, ed, 1896

The silliest woman can manage a clever man, but it takes a very clever woman to manage a fool.

➤ RUDYARD KIPLING,
Plain Tales from the Hills, 1888

It is best to love wisely, no doubt: but to love foolishly is better than not to be able to love at all.

➤ WILLIAM MAKEPEACE THACKERAY,
Pendennis, 1848

(See also *Blind Love, Changeable Love, Falling in Love, First Love, Forbidden Love, Love, Young Love*)

Forbidden Love

A demon's day in madness kissed
I swear I never had it like this
Forbidden yet I cannot resist.

➤ MELISSA ETHERIDGE,
"Resist," 1993

(See also *Enduring Love, Falling in Love, Famous Lovers, First Love, Foolish Love, Free Love, Love, Love at First Sight, Loving, Mature Love, Memories of Love, True Love, Unrequited Love, Young Love*)

 *Forgiveness*

Forgiveness is the act of admitting we are like other people.
— CHRISTINA BALDWIN,
Life's Companion, 1990

Love is an act of endless forgiveness, a tender look which becomes a habit.
— PETER USTINOV,
Christian Science Monitor, December 9, 1958

Who understands much, forgives much.
— MADAME DE STÄEL,
Corrine, 1807

Our heart is a treasury; if you spend all its wealth at once you are ruined. We find it as difficult to forgive a person for displaying his feeling in all its nakedness as we do to forgive a man for being penniless.
— HONORÉ DE BALZAC,
Le Pere Goriot, 1835

We pardon to the extent that we love.
— DUC DE LA ROCHEFOUCAULD,
Maximes, 1678

Once a woman has forgiven her man, she must not reheat his sins for breakfast.
— MARLENE DIETRICH,
Marlene Dietrich's ABC, 1962

 *Freedom*

Too much freedom is its own kind of cage.
—PATRICIA MACDONALD,
   Secret Admirer, 1995

Women, like men, ought to have their youth so glutted with freedom they hate the very idea of freedom.
—VITA SACKVILLE-WEST,
   letter, June 1, 1919,
   quoted in *Portrait of a Marriage* by Nigel Nicolson, 1973

Love will not always linger longest
With those who hold it in too clenched a fist.
—ALICE DUER MILLER,
   Forsaking All Others, 1931

If I have freedom in my love,
And in my soul am free,
Angels alone that soar above
Enjoy such liberty.
—RICHARD LOVELACE,
   "Lucasta," 1649

He loves to sit and hear me sing,
Then, laughing, sports and plays with me;
Then stretches out my golden wing,
And mocks my loss of liberty.
—WILLIAM BLAKE,
   "How Sweet I Roamed," *Poetical Sketches*, 1783

(See also *Free Love, Independence*)

Free Love

Free love is too expensive.
— BERNADETTE DEVLIN,
The Price of My Soul, 1969

(See also *First Love, Foolish Love, Forbidden Love, Love, Love at First Sight, Loving, Mature Love, Memories of Love, True Love, Unrequited Love, Young Love*)

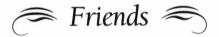

Friends

Each friend represents a world in us a world possibly not born until they arrive, and it is only by this meeting that a new world is born.
— ANAIS NIN,
The Diary of Anais Nin, 1967

I love everything that's old: old friends, old times, old manners, old books, old wines.
— OLIVER GOLDSMITH,
She Stoops to Conquer, 1773

From quiet homes and first beginning,
Out to the undiscovered ends,
There's nothing worth the wear of winning,
But laughter and the love of friends.
— JOACHIM DU BELLAY,
Dedicatory Ode, 1560

A friend loveth at all times.
　　　　➤ Proverbs 17:17

The ornament of a house is the friends who frequent it.
　　　➤ RALPH WALDO EMERSON,
　　　　Domestic Life, 1870

Can miles truly separate us from friends? If we want to be with someone we love, aren't we already there?
　　　➤ RICHARD BACH,
　　　　There's No Such Place as Far Away, 1994

Every one that flatters thee
Is no friend in misery.
Words are easy, like the wind;
Faithful friends are hard to find.
　　　➤ RICHARD BARNFIELD,
　　　　"In Divers Humours," 1598

Men and women can't be friends because the sex part always gets in the way.
　　　➤ NORA EPHRON,
　　　　When Harry Met Sally, 1989

Love begins with love, and the warmest friendship cannot change even to the coldest love.
　　　➤ JEAN DE LA BRUYERE,
　　　　Les Caracteres ou les moeurs de ce siecle, 1688

Friendship is Love without his wings!
　　　➤ LORD BYRON,
　　　　"L'Amitié," *Hours of Idleness*, 1806

A man's friendships are, like his will, invalidated by marriage—But they are also no less invalidated by the marriage of his friends.
　　　➤ SAMUEL BUTLER,
　　　　The Way of All Flesh, 1903

Greater love hath no man than this, that a man lay down his life for his friends.

➤ John 15:13

Friendship is certainly the finest balm for the pangs of disappointed love.

➤ JANE AUSTEN,
Northanger Abbey, 1818

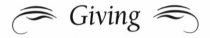 *Giving*

You give but little when you give of your possessions. It is when you give of yourself that you truly give.

➤ GIBRAN KHALIL GIBRAN,
The Prophet, 1923

A diamond is forever.

➤ FRANCES GERETY,
ad slogan for De Beers Consolidated Mines, 1940

Men are always better at offering women things that men like...and possibly one reason why women value flowers so much is because they must have been chosen simply to please her.

➤ KATHARINE WHITEHORN,
Roundabout, 1962

Why is it no one ever sent me yet
One perfect limousine, do you suppose?
Ah now, it's always just my luck to get
One perfect rose.

➤ DOROTHY PARKER,
"One Perfect Rose," 1937

I never hated a man enough to give him his diamonds back.

━ZSA ZSA GABOR,
Observer, August 25, 1957

So I really think that American gentlemen are the best after all, because kissing your hand may make you feel very very good, but a diamond and sapphire bracelet lasts forever.

━ANITA LOOS,
Gentlemen Prefer Blondes, 1925

 *God*

Liszt said to me today that God alone deserves to be loved. It may be true, but when one has loved a man it is very difficult to love God. It is so different.

━GEORGE SAND,
The Intimate Journal of George Sand, 1929

(See also *Christianity, Religion*)

 *Gossip*

Be thou as chaste as ice, as pure as snow, thou shalt not escape calumny.

━WILLIAM SHAKESPEARE,
Hamlet, 1601

Men have always detested women's gossip because they suspect the truth: their measurements are being taken and compared.

—ERICA JONG,
Fear of Flying, 1973

 *Great Love*

Great loves too must be endured.

—COCO CHANEL,
Coco Chanel, 1972

It was a great holiness, a religion, as all great loves must be.

—ELSIE DE WOLFE,
After All, 1935

Great loves were almost always great tragedies. Perhaps it was because love was never truly great until the element of sacrifice entered into it.

—MARY ROBERTS RINEHART,
Dangerous Days, 1919

In a great romance, each person basically plays a part that the other really likes.

—ELIZABETH ASHLEY,
The San Francisco Chronicle, 1982

There is a love that begins in the head, and goes down to the heart, and grows slowly; but it lasts till death, and asks less than it gives. There is another love, that blots out wisdom, that is sweet with the sweetness of life and bitter with the bitterness of death, lasting for an hour, but it is worth having lived a whole life for that hour.

—RALPH IRON,
The Story of an African Farm, 1883

Any great love involves sacrifice. You feel that as a father, as a husband. You give up all your freedom. But the love is so much greater than the freedom.

➤NICHOLAS CAGE,
The Times, June 17, 1998

(See also *Enduring Love, First Love, Foolish Love, Forbidden Love, Free Love, Love, Love at First Sight, Loving, Mature Love, Memories of Love, True Love, Young Love*)

 *Hair*

Fair tresses man's imperial race ensnare,
And beauty draws us with a single hair.

➤ALEXANDER POPE,
"The Rape of the Lock," 1714

Only God, my dear,
Could love you for yourself alone
And not your yellow hair.

➤W. B. YEATS,
"Anne Gregory," 1932

(See also *Appearance, Attraction, Beauty*)

Happiness

A man enjoys the happiness he feels, a woman the happiness she gives.

— PIERRE CHODERLOS DE LACLOS,
  Les Liaisons Dangereuses, 1782

I couldn't stand a happiness that went on morning noon and night...I promise to be a splendid husband, but give me a wife who, like the moon, does not rise every night in my sky.

— ANTON CHEKHOV,
  letter, March 23, 1895

It's afterwards you realize that the feeling of happiness you had with a man didn't necessarily prove that you loved him.

— MARGUERITE DURAS,
  Practicalities, 1990

There is only one happiness in life, to love and be loved.

— GEORGE SAND,
  letter to Lina Calamatta, March 31, 1862

(See also *Contentment*)

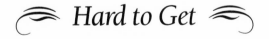

Hard to Get

She whom I love is hard to catch and conquer,
Hard, but O the glory of the winning were she won!

— GEORGE MEREDITH,
  "Love in the Valley," 1883

Never give all the heart, for love
Will hardly seem worth thinking of
To passionate women if it seem
Certain, and they never dream
That it fades out from kiss to kiss;
For everything that's lovely is
But a brief, dreamy kind delight
> ➤ W. B. YEATS,
> "In the Seven Woods," 1904

(See also *Falling in Love, First Love, Foolish Love, Forbidden Love, Free Love, Love, Memories of Love, Unrequited Love, Young Love*)

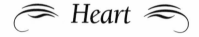 *Heart*

Nobody has ever measured, not even poets, how much the heart can hold.
> ➤ ZELDA FITZGERALD,
> *Zelda,* by Nancy Mitford, 1970

There are strings...in the human heart that had better not be vibrated.
> ➤ CHARLES DICKENS,
> *Barnaby Rudge,* 1841

The heart of another is a dark forest, always, no matter how close it has been to one's own.
> ➤ WILLA CATHER,
> *The Professor's House,* 1925

The door to the human heart can be opened only from the inside.
— Spanish proverb

Pity me that the heart is slow to learn
What the swift mind beholds at every turn.
— EDNA ST. VINCENT MILLAY,
"Pity Me Not," 1923

The heart has its reasons which reason knows nothing of.
— BLAISE PASCAL,
Pensees, 1670

The human heart, at whatever age, opens only to the heart that
opens in return.
— MARIA EDGEWORTH,
Letters to Literary Ladies, 1814

Two souls with but a single thought,
Two hearts that beat as one.
— FRIEDRICH HALM,
"Ingomar the Barbarian," *II Der Sohn der Wildness*, translated
by Marie Lovell, 1842

The desires of the heart are as crooked as corkscrews.
— W. H. AUDEN,
Death's Echo, 1937

It is only with the heart that one can see rightly; what is essential is
invisible to the eye.
— ANTOINE DE SAINT-EXUPERY,
The Little Prince, 1943

I know I am but summer to your heart
And not the full four seasons of the year.
— EDNA ST. VINCENT MILLAY,
"I Know I Am but Summer," *The Harp-Weaver*, 1923

The human heart likes a little disorder in its geometry.

—Louis de Bernieres,
Captain Corelli's Mandolin, 1994

(See also *First Love, Foolish Love, Forbidden Love, Free Love, Love, Love at First Sight, Loving, Mature Love, Memories of Love, True Love, Young Love*)

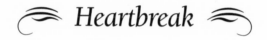

Heartbreak

Had we never lov'd sae kindly,
Had we never lov'd sae blindly
Never met—or never parted—
We had ne'er been broken-hearted.

—Robert Burns,
"Ae Fond Kiss," 1793

The lover who suffers not anguish knows not the worth of pleasure.

—Old Turkish proverb

The human heart does not stay away too long from that which hurt it most. There is a return journey to anguish that few of us are released from making.

—Lillian Smith,
The Journey, 1954

Well, since my baby left me
Well I found a new place to dwell
Well it's down at the end of lonely street
At Heartbreak Hotel.

—Elvis Presley,
"Heartbreak Hotel," 1956

I cannot say what loves have come and gone,
I only know that summer sang in me
A little while, that in me sings no more.

    ➤ EDNA ST. VINCENT MILLAY,
        "What Lips My Lips Have Kissed, and Where, and Why," *The Harp-Weaver*, 1923

Heaven has no rage like love to hatred turned,
Nor hell a fury, like a woman scorned.

    ➤ WILLIAM CONGREVE,
        "The Mourning Bride," 1697

My flocks feed not,
My ewes breed not,
My rams speed not,
All is amiss.
Love is dying,
Faith's defying,
Heart's denying,
Causer of this.

    ➤ RICHARD BARNFIELD,
        "A Shepherd's Complaint," 1626

It is difficult suddenly to put aside a long-standing love; it is difficult, but somehow you must do it.

    ➤ C. VALERIUS CATULLUS,
        Carmina, 1481

where have you one
with your confident
walk your
crooked smile the
rent money
in one pocket and
my heart in another.

    ➤ MARI E. EVANS,
        "Where Have You Gone," in *The Black Poets* by Dudley Randall, ed., 1971

Hearts will never be practical until they are made unbreakable.

➤L. FRANK BAUM,
The Wizard of Oz, 1939

When two people are under the influence of the most violent, most insane, most delusive, and most transient of passions, they are required to swear that they will remain in that excited, abnormal, and exhausting condition continuously until death do them part.

➤GEORGE BERNARD SHAW,
Getting Married, 1908

Never morning wore
To evening, but some heart did break.

➤ALFRED, LORD TENNYSON,
"In Memoriam A.H.H.," 1850

Pain
rusts into beauty, too
I know full well that this is so:
I had a heartbreak long ago

➤MARY CAROLYN DAVIES,
"Rust," *Youth Riding*, 1919

A broken heart is a very pleasant complaint for a man in London if he has a comfortable income.

➤GEORGE BERNARD SHAW,
Man and Superman, 1903

How do you know love has gone? If you said you would be there at seven and you get there by nine, and he or she has not called the police—it's gone.

➤MARLENE DIETRICH,
ABC, 1962

Hell, Madame, is to love no longer.

➤GEORGES BERNANOS,
The Diary of a Country Priest, 1936

Don't waste time trying to break a man's heart; be satisfied if you can just manage to chip it in a brand new place.

   —HELEN ROWLAND,
      A Guide to Men, 1922

The time you spend grieving over a man should never exceed the amount of time you actually spent with him.

   —DOROTHY L. SAYERS,
      Have His Carcase, 1942

Men have died from time to time, and worms have eaten them, but not for love.

   —WILLIAM SHAKESPEARE,
      As You Like It, 1599

Music I heard with you was more than music, and bread I broke with you was more than bread. Now that I am without you, all is desolate; all that was once so beautiful is dead.

   —CONRAD AIKEN,
      Bread and Music, 1914

'Tis better to have loved and lost than never to have loved at all.

   —Alfred, Lord Tennyson
      In Memoriam, 1850

'Tis not love's going hurts my days
But that it went in little ways.

   —EDNA ST. VINCENT MILLAY,
      "The Spring and the Fall" *The Harp-Weaver*, 1923

In the past, in old novels, the price of love was death, a price which virtuous women paid in childbirth, and the wicked, like Nana, was the pox. Nowadays it is paid in thrombosis or neurosis: one can take one's pick.

   —MARGARET DRABBLE,
      The Waterfall, 1969

O! Many a shaft, at random sent,
Finds mark the archer little meant!
And many a word, at random spoken,
May soothe or wound a heart that's broken.

> ➤Sir Walter Scott,
> "The Lord of the Isles," 1813

They say that men suffer,
As badly, as long.
I worry, I worry,
In case they are wrong.

> ➤Wendy Cope,
> "I Worry," 1992

Love's pleasure lasts but a moment; love's sorrow lasts all through life.

> ➤Jean-Pierre Claris de Florian,
> *Celestine*, 1784

Those who have the courage to love should have courage to suffer.

> ➤Anthony Trollope,
> *The Bertrams*, 1859

No thorns go as deep as a rose's,
And love is more cruel than lust.

> ➤Algernon Charles Swinburne,
> "Dolores," 1866

Those have most power to hurt us that we love.

> ➤Francis Beaumont and John Fletcher,
> *The Maid's Tragedy*, 1610

There are some meannesses which are too mean even for man—woman, lovely woman alone, can venture to commit them.

> ➤William Makepeace Thackeray,
> *A Shabby Genteel Story*, 1840

(See also *Blind Love, Changeable Love, End of Love, Enduring Love, Falling in Love, First Love, Foolish Love, Forbidden Love, Great Love, Love, Mature Love, Memories of Love, True Love, Unrequited Love, Young Love*)

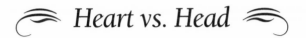

Heart vs. Head

There is a road from the eye to the heart that does not go through the intellect.

—G. K. CHESTERTON,
The Defendant, 1901

Four be the things I am wiser to know:
Idleness, sorrow, a friend, and a foe.
Four be the things I'd been better without:
Love, curiosity, freckles, and doubt.

—DOROTHY PARKER,
"Enough Rope," 1927

It's very hard to get your heart and head together in life. In my case, they're not even friendly.

—WOODY ALLEN,
Husbands and Wives, 1992

I am all for people having their heart in the right place, but the right place for a heart is not inside the head.

—KATHARINE WHITEHORN,
Roundabout, 1962

It is impossible to love and to be wise.

—FRANCIS BACON,
Essays, 1625

Never til Time is done
Will the fire of the heart and the fire of the mind be one.

➤ EDITH SITWELL,
quoted in *Edith Sitwell* by Elizabeth Salter and Allanah
Harper, eds., 1976

Well, love is insanity. The ancient Greeks knew that. It is the taking
over of a rational and lucid mind by delusion and self-destruction.
You lose yourself, you have no power over yourself, you can't even
think straight.

➤ MARILYN FRENCH,
The Women's Room, 1977

Any scientist who has ever been in love knows that he may understand everything about sex hormones but the actual experience is
something quite different.

➤ KATHLEEN LONSDALE,
Universities Quarterly, 1963

Love is the state in which man sees things most widely different
from what they are.... When a man is in love, he endures more
than at other times; he submits to everything.

➤ FRIEDRICH WILHELM NIETZSCHE,
The Antichrist, 1888

Fish gotta swim, birds gotta fly,
I gotta love one man till I die.
Can't help lovin' that man of mine.
Tell me he's lazy, tell me he's slow,
Tell me I'm crazy, maybe I know.

➤ OSCAR HAMMERSTEIN III,
"Can't Help Lovin' Dat Man," *Showboat*, 1928

A man is in general better pleased when he has a good dinner on
his table than when his wife talks Greek.

➤ SAMUEL JOHNSON,
quoted in *The Works of Samuel Johnson* by John Hawkins, ed.,
1787

(See also *Heart, Heartbreak, First Love, Foolish Love, Forbidden Love, Free Love, Love, Love at First Sight, Loving, Mature Love, Memories of Love, True Love, Unrequited Love, Young Love*)

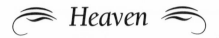 *Heaven*

Love rules the court, the camp, the grove,
And men below, and saints above;
For love is heaven, and heaven is love.
> —SIR WALTER SCOTT,
> *The Lay of the Last Minstrel*, 1805

I'm in heaven
And my heart beats so that I can hardly speak
When we're out together dancing cheek to cheek
> —IRVING BERLIN,
> "Cheek to Cheek," *Top Hat*, 1935

My girl, thou gaest much
upon the golden skies:
Would I were heaven! I would behold
thee with all mine eyes.
> —GEORGE TURBERVILLE,
> "The Lover to His Lady, that Gazed Much up to the Skies"

Marriages are made in heaven and consummated on earth.
> —JOHN LYLY,
> *Mother Bombie*, 1590

(See also *Christianity, God, Religion*)

 *Homosexuality*

No government has the right to tell its citizens when or whom to love. The only queer people are those who don't love anybody.

— RITA MAE BROWN,
   speech at the opening ceremony of the Gay Olympics, August 28, 1982

He was the wren and the rain, he was the wind and the trees bending under the wind. He was split in two, the mover and the moved, the male and the female.

— MARGARET MILLER,
   Beast in View, 1955

Sexual fidelity is more important in a homosexual relationship than in any other. In other relationships there are a variety of ties. But here, fidelity is the only bond.

— W. H. AUDEN,
   quoted in *Table Talk of W. H. Auden* by Nicholas Jenkins, ed., 1990

It is so true that a woman may be in love with a woman, and a man with a man. It is pleasant to be sure of it, because it is undoubtedly the same love that we shall feel when we are angels.

— MARGARET FULLER,
   quoted in *Margaret Fuller, Whetstone of Genius* by Mason Wade, 1940

Love is love. Gender is merely spare parts.

— WENDY WASSERSTEIN,
   The Sisters Rosensweig, 1991

It's funny how heterosexuals have lives and the rest of us have "lifestyles."

— SONIA JOHNSON,
   Going Out of Our Minds, 1987

I am the Love that dare not speak its name.
> ▬LORD ALFRED BRUCE DOUGLAS,
> *Two Loves*, 1894

(See also *Bisexuality, Lesbians*)

 *Honesty*

The one charm of marriage is that it makes a life of deception absolutely necessary for both parties.
> ▬OSCAR WILDE,
> *The Picture of Dorian Gray*, 1891

Perhaps there is no position more perilous to a man's honesty than that...of knowing himself to be quite loved by a girl whom he almost loves himself.
> ▬ANTHONY TROLLOPE,
> *Phineas Finn*, 1869

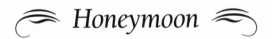 *Honeymoon*

When I first saw [Niagara] Falls, I was disappointed in the outline. Every American bride is taken there, and the sight must be one of the earliest, if not the keenest, disappointments in American married life.
> ▬OSCAR WILDE,
> New York press interview, 1882

Our honeymoon will shine our life long; its beams will only fade over your grave or mine.
　　⬤CHARLOTTE BRONTË,
　　　Jane Eyre, 1847

These days, the honeymoon is rehearsed much more often than the wedding.
　　⬤P. J. O'ROURKE,
　　　Modern Manners, 1984

(See also *Husband, Marriage, Wives*)

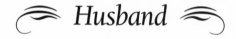

Husband

If you cannot have your dear husband for a comfort and a delight, for a breadwinner and a crosspatch, for a sofa, chair or a hot-water bottle, one can use him as a Cross to be Borne.
　　⬤STEVIE SMITH,
　　　Novel on Yellow Paper, 1936

You mean apart from my own?
　　⬤ZSA ZSA GABOR,
　　　when asked how many husbands she had had,
　　　quoted in *I Wish I'd Said That* by K. Edwards, 1976

A husband is what is left of a lover, after the nerve has been extracted.
　　⬤HELEN ROWLAND,
　　　A Guide to Men, 1922

Husbands, love your wives, and be not bitter against them.
　　⬤Colossians 3:19

A husband, like a government, never needs to admit a fault.
> ←Honoré de Balzac,
> *Physiology of Marriage*, 1829

So far as possible ensure that you allow your husband to come upon you only when there is delight in the meeting. Whenever the finances allow, the husband and wife should have separate bedrooms.
> ←Marie Stopes,
> *Married Love*, 1918

One reproaches a lover, but can one reproach a husband, when his only fault is that he no longer loves?
> ←Madame de la Fayette,
> *The Princess of Cleves*, 1678

No matter how liberated she is every woman still wants a husband.
> ←P. J. O'Rourke,
> *Modern Manners*, 1984

If ever two were one, then surely we.
If ever man were loved by wife, then thee;
If ever wife was happy in a man,
Compare with me ye women if you can.
> ←Anne Bradstreet,
> "To My Dear and Loving Husband," 1678

The kind of man that *men* like—not women—is the kind of man that makes the best husband.
> ←Frank Norris,
> *The Pit*, 1903

Women love scallywags, but some marry them and then try to make them wear a blazer.
> ←David Bailey,
> *Mail on Sunday*, February 16, 1997

Being a husband is a whole-time job. That is why so many husbands fail. They cannot give their entire attention to it.

—ARNOLD BENNETT,
The Title, 1918

He looked homemade, as though his wife had self-consciously knitted or somehow contrived a husband when she sat alone at night.

—EUDORA WELTY,
A Curtain of Green, 1941

(See also *Honeymoon, Marriage, Wives*)

Imagination

The lunatic, the lover, and the poet,
Are of imagination all compact.

—WILLIAM SHAKESPEARE,
A Midsummer Night's Dream, 1595

It would seem that love never seeks real perfection, and even fears it. It delights only in the perfection it has itself imagined.

—NICOLAS-SEBASTIEN CHAMFORT,
Maximes et Pensees, 1796

Were it not for imagination, Sir, a man would be as happy in the arms of a chambermaid as of a Duchess.

—SAMUEL JOHNSON,
quoted in *Life of Johnson* by James Boswell, May 9, 1778

Let us leave pretty women to men devoid of imagination.

—MARCEL PROUST,
Remembrance of Things Past, 1922–1931

If a bloke asks me the time of day often enough, after a while I only have to look at my watch to imagine myself saying "I Do" and driving a Volvo Estate filled with children dressed in Baby Gap clothes.

━ARABELLA WEIR,
Does My Bum Look Big in This?, 1997

It is the terrible deception of love that it begins by engaging us in play not with a woman of the external world but with a doll fashioned in our brain—the only woman moreover that we have always at our disposal, the only one we shall ever possess.

━MARCEL PROUST,
The Guermantes Way, 1921

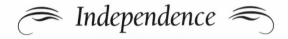 *Independence*

"Once the realization is accepted that even between the closest human beings infinite distances continue to exist, a wonderful living side by side can grow up, if they succeed in loving the distance between them which makes it possible for each to see the other whole and against a wide sky."

━RAINER MARIA RILKE,
in *Letters to a Young Poet*, 1934

I dream that love without tyranny is possible.

━ANDREA DWORKIN,
"First Love," in *The Woman Who Lost Her Names* by Julia Wolf Mazow, ed., 1980

No human relation gives one possession in another—every two souls are absolutely different. In friendship or in love, the two side by side raise hands together to find what one cannot reach alone.

━KAHLIL GIBRAN,
Beloved Prophet: The Love Letters of Kahlil Gibran and Mary Haskell and her private journal, 1972

We love in another's soul
whatever of ourselves
we can deposit in it;
the greater the deposit;
the greater the love.
> ➤ IRVING LAYTON,
> "Aphs," 1969

I leave before being left. I decide.
> ➤ BRIGITTE BARDOT,
> *Newsweek*, March 5, 1973

Oh, I hate a lover that can dare to think he draws a moment's air independent on the bounty of his mistress.
> ➤ WILLIAM CONGREVE,
> *The Way of the World*, 1700

If I'm ever to reach any understanding of myself and the things around me, I must learn to stand alone. That's why I can't stay here with you any longer.
> ➤ Nora in *A Doll's House*
> by HENRIK IBSEN, 1879

The meeting of two personalities is like the contact of two chemical substances: if there is any reaction, both are transformed.
> ➤ CARL JUNG,
> *Modern Man in Search of a Soul*, 1933

I love you so passionately that I hide a great part of my love, not to oppress you with it.
> ➤ MARIE DE RABUTIN-CHANTAL, MARQUISE DE SEVIGNE,
> *Letters of Mme. de Sevigne to Her Daughter and Her Friends*,
> vol. 1, 1811

(See also *Freedom, Free Love, Individuality*)

 *Individuality*

The boughs of no two trees ever have the same arrangement. Nature always produces individuals, she never produces classes.
  ━LYDIA MARIA CHILD,
    Letters from New York, 1845

Life has taught us that love does not consist in gazing at each other but in looking outward together in the same direction.
  ━ANTOINE DE SAINT-EXUPERY,
    Wind, Sand, and Stars, 1939

(See also *Freedom, Free Love, Independence*)

 *Infidelity*

There are plenty of men who philander during the summer, to be sure, but they are usually the same lot who philander during the winter—albeit with less convenience.
  ━NORA EPHRON,
    New York Post, August 22, 1965

I never was attached to that great sect
Whose doctrine is that each one should select
Out of the crowd a mistress or a friend,
And all the rest, though fair and wise, commend
To cold oblivion.
  ━PERCY BYSSHE SHELLEY,
    Epipsychidion, 1821

In matters of love men's eyes are always bigger than their bellies. They have violent appetites, 'tis true; but they have soon dined.
　　►JOHN VANBRUGH,
　　　　Relapse, 1696

I can't fool you—and yet I would like to. I mean that I can never be absolutely loyal—it's not in me. I love women, or life, too much—which it is, I don't know.
　　►HENRY MILLER,
　　　　letter to Anais Nin, March 21, 1932

Wouldn't that be like shoplifting in a secondhand store?
　　►JEAN HARLOW,
　　　　when asked if she would steal a husband,
　　　　quoted in *Harlow* by Irving Shulman, 1964

A father will have compassion on his son. A mother will never forget her child. A brother will cover the sin of his sister. But what husband ever forgave the faithlessness of his wife?
　　►MARGUERITE D'ANGOULEME,
　　　　Mirror of the Sinful Soul, 1531

For men, infidelity is not inconstancy.
　　►PIERRE CHODERLOS DE LACLOS,
　　　　Les Liaisons Dangereuses, 1782

After the door of a woman's heart has once swung on its silent hinges, a man thinks he can prop it open with a brick and go away and leave it.
　　►MYRTLE REED,
　　　　The Spinster Book, 1901

Your idea of fidelity is not having more than one man in bed at the same time.
　　►FREDERIC RAPHAEL,
　　　　Dating, 1965

It is easier to keep half a dozen lovers guessing than to keep one lover after he has stopped guessing.

— HELEN ROWLAND,
　　Reflections of a Bachelor Girl, 1903

It is better to be unfaithful than faithful without wanting to be.

— BRIGITTE BARDOT,
　　"Sayings of the Week," *The Observer*, February 18, 1968

Translations (like wives) are seldom strictly faithful if they are in the least attractive.

— ROY CAMPBELL,
　　Poetry Review, June–July 1949

People who are so dreadfully "devoted" to their wives are so apt, from mere habit, to get devoted to other people's wives as well.

— JANE WELSH CARLYLE,
　　quoted in *Letters and Memorials of Jane Welsh Carlyle* by
　　James Anthony Froude, ed., 1883

Love is a boaster at heart, who cannot hide the stolen horse without giving a glimpse of the bridle.

— MARY RENAULT,
　　The Last of the Wine, 1956

Why should marriage bring only tears?
All I wanted was a man
With a single heart,
And we would stay together
As our hair turned white,
Not somebody always after wriggling fish
With his big bamboo rod

— CHUO WEN-CHUN,
　　quoted in *The Orchid Boat* by Kenneth Rexroth and Ling
　　Chung, eds., 1972

(See also *Affairs, Betrayal*)

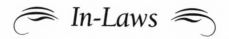 *In-Laws*

I should, many a good day, have blown my brains out, but for the recollection that it would have given pleasure to my mother-in-law; and even then, if I could have been certain to haunt her...
> ⟵LORD BYRON,
> letter, January 28, 1817

The ideal is to marry an orphan.
> ⟵JILLY COOPER,
> *How to Stay Married,* 1977

I was a post-war, utility son-in-law! Not quite the Frog-Prince. Maybe the Swineherd.
> ⟵TED HUGHES,
> *Birthday Letters,* 1998

(See also *Marriage*)

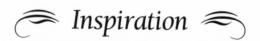 *Inspiration*

Our chief want in life is somebody who will make us do what we can.
> ⟵RALPH WALDO EMERSON,
> *Considerations by the Way,* 1860

In our life there is a single color, as on an artist's palette, which provides the meaning of life and art. It is the color of love.
> ⟵MARC CHAGALL,
> *Newsweek,* April 8, 1985

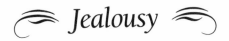 *Jealousy*

Oh! How bitter a thing it is to look into happiness through another man's eyes.

> —WILLIAM SHAKESPEARE,
> *As You Like It*, 1599

Jealousy in romance is like salt in food. A little can enhance the savor, but too much can spoil their pleasure and, under certain circumstances, can be life-threatening.

> —MAYA ANGELOU,
> *Wouldn't Take Nothing for My Journey New*, 1993

Jealousy had a taste all right. A bitter and tongue-stinging flavor, like a peach pit.

> —DOLORES HITCHENS,
> *In a House Unknown*, 1973

Jealousy, that dragon which slays love under the pretence of keeping it alive.

> —HAVELOCK ELLIS,
> *On Life and Sex: Essays of Love and Virtue*, 1937

People may go on talking forever of the jealousies of pretty women; but for real genuine hard-working envy, there is nothing like an ugly woman with a taste for admiration.

> —EMILY EDEN,
> *The Semi-Attached Couple*, 1830

Never has jealousy added to character, never does it make the individual big and fine.

> —EMMA GOLDMAN,
> "Jealousy: Causes and a Possible Cure," in *Real Emma Speaks*
> by Alix Kates Shulman, ed., 1985

Anger and jealousy can no more bear to lose sight of their objects than love.

➤ GEORGE ELIOT,
The Mill on the Floss, 1860

Jealousy is no more than feeling alone against smiling enemies.

➤ ELIZABETH BOWEN,
The House in Paris, 1935

I believe she would be jealous of a fine day if her husband praised it.

➤ HANNAH MORE,
Coelebs in Search of a Wife, 1808

The jealous bring down the curse they fear upon their own heads.

➤ DOROTHY DIX,
Dorothy Dix—Her Book, 1926

Inquisitiveness as seldom cures jealousy, as drinking in a fever quenches the thirst.

➤ WILLIAM WYCHERLEY,
Love in a Wood, 1672

It is the green-eyed monster which doth mock the meat it feeds on.

➤ WILLIAM SHAKESPEARE,
Othello, 1602

Kisses

Jenny kissed me when we met,
Jumping from the chair she sat in;
Time, you thief, who love to get
Sweets into your list, put that in:
Say I'm weary, say I'm sad,
Say that health and wealth have missed me,
Say I'm growing old, but add,
Jenny kissed me.

— LEIGH HUNT,
   "Rondeau," 1838

I was born when she kissed me. I died when she left me. I lived a few weeks while she loved me.

— HUMPHREY BOGART,
   quoted in *A Lonely Place* by Andrew Solt, 1950

Where do the noses go? I always wondered where the noses would go.

— ERNEST HEMINGWAY,
   For Whom the Bell Tolls, 1940

Was this the face that launched a thousand ships? And burnt the topless towers of Ilium? Sweet Helen, make me immortal with a kiss!

— CHRISTOPHER MARLOWE,
   The Tragical History of the Life and Death of Dr. Faustus,
   c 1592

But his kiss was so sweet, and so closely he pressed,
That I languished and pined til I granted the rest.

— JOHN GAY,
   The Beggar's Opera, 1728

First time he kissed me, he but only kissed
The fingers of this hand wherewith I write;
And, ever since, it grew more clean and white.
➤ ELIZABETH BARRETT BROWNING,
Sonnets from the Portuguese, 1850

Being kissed by a man who didn't wax his moustache was—like
eating an egg without salt.
➤ RUDYARD KIPLING,
The Story of the Gadsbys, 1889

Teach not thy lip such scorn, for it was made
For kissing, lady, not for such contempt.
➤ WILLIAM SHAKESPEARE,
King Richard III, 1592

Love at the lips was touch
As sweet as I could bear;
And once that seemed too much;
I lived on air.
➤ ROBERT FROST,
"To Earthward," 1923

You must remember this:
A kiss is just a kiss,
A sigh is just a sigh;
The fundamental things apply,
As time goes by.

And when two lovers woo,
They still say, "I love you";
On that you can rely,
No matter what the future brings
➤ HERMAN HUPFELD,
"As Time Goes By," 1931

Let him kiss me with the kisses of his mouth: for thy love is better than wine.

   ←Song of Solomon 1:2

What is a kiss? Why this, as some approve:
The sure, sweet cement, glue and lime of love.

   ←ROBERT HERRICK,
      "A Kiss," 1648

Suns may set and rise again: for us, when our brief light has set, there's the sleep of one ever lasting night. Give me a thousand kisses.

   ←CAIUS VALERIUS CATULLUS,
      Carmina

Lord, I wonder what fool it was that first invented kissing!

   ←JONATHAN SWIFT,
      Polite Conversation, 1738

And the sunlight clasps the earth,
And the moonbeams kiss the sea—
What are all these kissings worth,
If thou kiss not me?

   ←PERCY BYSSHE SHELLEY,
      "Love's Philosophy," 1819

A man had given all other bliss,
And all his worldly worth for this,
To waste his whole heart in one kiss
Upon her perfect lips.

   ←ALFRED, LORD TENNYSON,
      "Sir Launcelot and Queen Guinevere," 1842

You should not take a fellow eight years old and make him swear
to never kiss the girls.
ROBERT BROWNING,
Fra Lippo Lippi, 1855

She press'd his hand in slumber; so once more
He could not help but kiss her and adore.
—JOHN KEATS,
Endymion, 1818

But kiss: one kiss! Rubies unparagoned,
How dearly they do't!
—WILLIAM SHAKESPEARE,
Cymbeline, 1609–1610

I smoked my first cigarette and kissed my first woman on the same
day. I have never had time for tobacco since.
—ARTURO TOSCANINI,
Observer, June 30, 1946

When you kiss me
jaguars lope through my knees
when you kiss me,
my lips quiver like bronze
violets; oh, when you kiss me
—DIANE ACKERMAN,
"Beija-Flor," *Jaguar of Sweet Laughter*, 1991

If love is the best thing in life, then the best part of love is the kiss.
—THOMAS MANN,
Lotte in Weimar, 1939

I kissed thee ere I killed thee, no way but this,
Killing myself to die upon a kiss.
—WILLIAM SHAKESPEARE,
Othello, 1602

Now a soft kiss—Aye, by that kiss, I vow an endless bliss
— JOHN KEATS,
   Endymion, 1818

 Lesbians

Are there many things in this cool-hearted world so utterly exquisite as the pure love of one woman for another woman?
— MARY MACLANE,
   The Story of Mary MacLane, 1902

I will be quiet, be still, and know that it is God who put the love for women in my heart.
— BRIGITTE ROBERTS,
   "Be Still and Know," in *Women on Women* by Naomi Holoch and Joan Nestle, eds., 1993

A woman
who loves a woman
is forever young
— ANNE SEXTON,
   "Rapunzel," *Transformations,* 1971

(See also *Bisexuality, Homosexuals*)

 Life

Life loves the liver of it.
— MAYA ANGELOU,
   Conversations with Maya Angelou, 1989

Is it so small a thing
To have enjoyed the sun,
To have lived light in the spring,
To have loved, to have thought, to have done?
　　➤MATTHEW ARNOLD,
　　　Empedocles on Etna, 1852

Dost thou love life? Then do not squander time; for that's the stuff
life is made of.
　　➤BENJAMIN FRANKLIN,
　　　Poor Richard's Almanac, 1746

In the life of each of us, I said to myself, there is a place remote and
islanded, and given to endless regret or secret happiness.
　　➤SARAH ORNE JEWETT,
　　　The Country of the Pointed Firs, 1896

Love...
That cordial drop heaven in our cup has thrown
To make the nauseous draught of life go down.
　　➤LORD ROCHESTER,
　　　letter from Artemisia in the Town to Chloe in the Country,
　　　1679

To live is like to love—all reason is against it, and all healthy
instinct for it.
　　➤SAMUEL BUTLER,
　　　"Life and Love," *Notebooks*, 1912

Let your boat of life be light, packed with only what you need—a
homely home and simple pleasures, one or two friends, worth the
name, someone to love and someone to love you, a cat, a dog, and
a pipe or two, enough to eat and enough to wear, and a little more
than enough to drink; for thirst is a dangerous thing.
　　➤JEROME K. JEROME,
　　　Three Men in a Boat, 1889

I don't want to live—I want to love first, and live incidentally.

——ZELDA FITZGERALD,
  quoted in *Zelda* by Nancy Mitford, 1970

 Living Together

It is not time or opportunity that is to determine intimacy; it is disposition alone. Seven year would be insufficient to make some people acquainted with each other, and seven days are more than enough for others.

——JANE AUSTEN,
  Sense and Sensibility, 1811

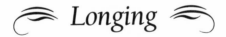 Longing

Is there anything better than to be longing for something, when you know it is within reach?

——GRETA GARBO,
  quoted in *The Divine Garbo* by Frederick Sands and
  Sven Broman, 1979

Three passions, simple but overwhelmingly strong, have governed my life: the longing for love, the search for knowledge, and unbearable pity for the suffering of mankind.

—BERTRAND RUSSELL,
Autobiography, 1967

(See also *Desire, Passion*)

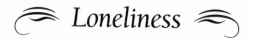

Loneliness

Love all the people you can. The sufferings from love are not to be compared to the sorrows of loneliness.

—SUSAN HALE,
quoted in *Letters of Susan Hale* by Caroline P. Atkinson, ed.,
1918

Lonely people talking to each other can make each other lonelier.

—LILLIAN HELLMAN,
The Autumn Garden, 1951

Oh, please have some pity
I'm all alone in this big city
I tell you I'm just a lonesome babe in the wood,
So lady be good to me.

—IRA GERSHWIN,
Oh, Lady Be Good, 1926

(See also *Alone*)

 # Love

She deserves
More worlds than I can lose.
— JOHN DRYDEN,
"All for Love," 1678

Whoever has loved knows all that life contains of sorrow and of joy.
— GEORGE SAND,
French Wit and Wisdom, 1950

Is it prickly to touch as a hedge is,
Or soft as eiderdown fluff?
Is it sharp or quite smooth at the edges?
O tell me the truth about love.
— W. H. AUDEN,
"Oh Tell Me the Truth About Love," 1938

One hour of right-down love
Is worth an age of dully living on.
— APHRA BEHN,
quoted in *Uncommon Scold* by Abby Adams, 1989

Down on your knees, and thank heaven, fasting, for a good man's love.
— WILLIAM SHAKESPEARE,
As You Like It, 1600

Love has its own instinct. It knows how to find the road to the heart just as the weakest insect moves toward its flower by an irresistible will which fears nothing.
— HONORÉ DE BALZAC,
La Femme de Trente Ans, 1832

I go where I love and where I am loved.

> ━H. D.,
> *The Flowering of the Rod*, 1946

I believe in the curative powers of love as the English believe in tea or Catholics believe in the Miracle of Lourdes.

> ━LOYCE JOHNSON,
> *Minor Characters*, 1983

I always wanted to be in love, always. It's like being a tuning fork.

> ━EDNA O'BRIEN,
> "Diary of an Unfaithful Wife," *Cosmopolitan*, 1966

Love is the bright foreigner, the foreign self.

> ━RALPH WALDO EMERSON,
> *Essays*, 1841

Come live with me and be my love,
And we will all the pleasures prove
That hills and valleys, dales and fields,
Woods, or steepy mountain yields.

> ━CHRISTOPHER MARLOWE,
> "The Passionate Shepherd to His Love," 1589

Whoso loves
Believes the impossible

> ━ELIZABETH BARRETT BROWNING,
> *Aurora Leigh*, 1857

Love's but the frailty of the mind, when 'tis not with ambition joined.

> ━WILLIAM CONGREVE,
> *The Way of the World*, 1700

It is the same in love as in war; a fortress that parleys is half taken.

> ━ MARGUERITE DE VALOIS,
> *Memoirs*, 1628

People talk about love as though it were something you could give, like an armful of flowers. And a lot of people give love like that— just dump it down on top of you, a useless strong-scented burden.

    —ANNE MORROW LINDBERG,
      Locked Rooms and Open Doors, 1974

A smile that glowed
Celestial rosy red
Love's proper hue.

    —JOHN MILTON,
      Paradise Lost, 1667

Freely we serve
Because we freely love, as in our will
To love or not; in this we stand or fall.

    —JOHN MILTON,
      Paradise Lost, 1667

Love is enough: though the world be a-waning,
And the woods have no voice but the voice of complaining.

    —WILLIAM MORRIS,
      "Love Is Enough," 1872

My love is of a birth as rare
As 'tis, for object, strange and high;
It was begotten by despair, Upon impossibility.

    —ANDREW MARVELL,
      "The Definition of Love," 1652

I guess what everyone wants more than anything else is to be loved.

    —ELLA FITZGERALD,
      in *Newsweek*, June 7, 1954

Where love is concerned, too much is not ever enough.

    —PIERRE DE BEAUMARCHAIS,
      Marriage of Figaro, 1784

Love doesn't just sit there, like a stone, it has to be made, like bread; remade all the time, made new.

➤ URSULA LE GUIN,
  The Lathe of Heaven, 1971

Under yonder beech-tree single on the greensward,
Couched with her arms behind her golden head,
Knees and tresses folded to slip and ripple idly,
Lies my young love sleeping in the shade.

➤ GEORGE MEREDITH,
  "Love in the Valley," 1883

Where love rules, there is no will to power; and where power predominates, there love is lacking. The one is the shadow of the other.

➤ CARL JUNG,
  The Psychology of the Unconscious, 1943

And now these three remain: faith, hope and love. But the greatest of these is love.

➤ 1 Corinthians 13:13

Two persons love in one another the future good which they aid one another to unfold.

➤ MARGARET FULLER,
  Women in the Nineteenth Century, 1845

It is those we live with and love and should know who elude us.

➤ NORMAN MACLEAN,
  A River Runs Through It, 1976

All thoughts, all passions, all delights,
Whatever stirs this mortal frame,
All are but ministers of Love,
And feed his sacred flame.

➤ SAMUEL TAYLOR COLERIDGE,
  "Love," 1799

Flowers are lovely; love is flower-like;
Friendship is a sheltering tree.

    SAMUEL TAYLOR COLERIDGE,
      "Youth and Age," 1832

He prayeth best, who loveth best
All things both great and small;
For the dear God who loveth us,
He made and loveth all.

    SAMUEL TAYLOR COLERIDGE,
      The Ancient Mariner, 1798

Love consists in this, that two solitudes protect and touch and greet each other.

    RAINER MARIA RILKE,
      Letters to a Young Poet, 1987

So often when we say "I love you" we say it with a huge "I" and a small "you."

    ANTONY, RUSSIAN ORTHODOX ARCHBISHOP OF ENGLAND,
      Beginning to Pray, 1970

How do I love thee? Let me count the ways.
I love thee to the depth and breadth and height
My soul can reach, when feeling out of sight
For the ends of Being and ideal Grace.

    ELIZABETH BARRETT BROWNING,
      Sonnets from the Portuguese, 1850

There is only one happiness in life: to love and be loved.

    GEORGE SAND,
      letter to Lina Calamatta, March 31, 1862

Life in common among people who love each other is the ideal of happiness.

    GEORGE SAND,
      Histoire de Ma Vie, 1856

Love and a cough cannot be hid.
➤ GEORGE HERBERT,
Jacula Prudentum, 1651

Love bade me welcome; yet my soul drew back
Guilty of dust and sin.
➤ GEORGE HERBERT,
"Love," *Temple* 1633

Look for me by moonlight;
Watch for me by moonlight;
I'll come to thee by moonlight,
Though hell should bar the way!
➤ ALFRED NOYES,
The Highwayman, 1907

Love your neighbour, yet pull not down your hedge.
➤ GEORGE HERBERT,
Jacula Prudentum, 1651

We loved, sir—used to meet:
How sad and bad and mad it was—
But then, how it was sweet!
➤ ROBERT BROWNING,
"Confessions," 1864

Oh, when I was in love with you,
Then I was clean and brave.
➤ A. E. HOUSMAN,
A Shropshire Lad, 1896

Love to faults is always blind,
Always is to joy inclin'd,
Lawless, wing'd and unconfin'd,
And breaks all chains from every mind.
➤ WILLIAM BLAKE,
"Love to Faults," *Poems from Blake's Notebook*, 1792

Here of a Sunday morning
My love and I would lie,
and see the coloured counties,
And hear the larks so high
About us in the sky.
>   ◄─A. E. HOUSMAN,
>   *A Shropshire Lad*, 1896

It seemed to me pretty plain, that they had more of love than matrimony in them.
>   ◄─OLIVER GOLDSMITH,
>   *The Vicar of Wakefield*, 1766

A lover without indiscretion is no lover at all.
>   ◄─THOMAS HARDY,
>   *The Hand of Ethelberta*, 1876

There isn't any formula or method. You learn to love by loving—by paying attention and doing what one thereby discovers has to be done.
>   ◄─ALDOUS HUXLEY,
>   *Time Must Have a Stop*, 1944

Proud word you never spoke, but you will speak
For not exempt from pride some future day.
Resting on one white hand a warm wet cheek
Over my open volume you will say,
"This man loved me!" then rise and trip away.
>   ◄─WALTER SAVAGE LANDOR,
>   **"Proud Word You Never Spoke,"** 1853

Does the Eagle know what is in the pit
Or wilt thou go ask the Mole?
Can Wisdom be put in a silver rod,
Or Love in a golden bowl?
>   ◄─WILLIAM BLAKE,
>   *The Book of Thel*, 1792

For Mercy has a human heart,
Pity a human face,
And Love, the human form divine,
And Peace, the human dress.
> ◂WILLIAM BLAKE,
> "The Divine Image," *Songs of Innocence*, 1790

Love seeketh not itself to please,
Nor for itself hath any care,
But for another gives its ease,
And builds a Heaven in Hell's despair.
> ◂WILLIAM BLAKE,
> "The Clod and the Pebble," *Songs of Experience*, 1794

There is always something left to love. And if you haven't learned that, you ain't learned nothing.
> ◂LORRAINE HANSBERRY,
> *A Raisin in the Sun*, 1959

Love is much nicer to be in than an automobile accident, a tight girdle, a higher tax bracket or a holding pattern over Philadelphia.
> ◂JUDITH VIORST,
> *Redbook*, 1975

Twice or thrice had I loved thee,
Before I knew thy face or name.
> ◂JOHN DONNE,
> "Air and Angels," 1633

Love, all alike, no season knows, nor clime,
Nor hours, days, months, which are the rags of time.
> ◂JOHN DONNE,
> "The Sun Rising," 1633

And love's the noblest frailty of the mind.
> ◂JOHN DRYDEN,
> "The Indian Emperor," 1667

Only our love hath no decay;
This, no tomorrow hath, nor yesterday,
Running it never runs from us away,
But truly keeps his first, last,
everlasting day.

> —JOHN DONNE,
> "The Anniversary," 1611

Never love unless you can
Bear with all the faults of man.

> —THOMAS CAMPION,
> *Third Book of Airs*, 1617

There is a lady sweet and kind,
Was never face so pleased my mind;
I did but see her passing by,
And yet I love her till I die.

> —THOMAS FORD,
> "There Is a Lady," 1607

In how many lives does love really play a dominant part? The average taxpayer is no more capable of the grand passion than of a grand opera.

> —ISRAEL ZANGWILL,
> *Who Said That?*, BBC TV, February 11, 1958

Love's a thin diet, nor will keep out cold.

> —APHRA BEHN,
> *The Lucky Chance*, 1686

I thought well as well him as another and then I asked him with my eyes to ask again yes and then he asked me would I yes to say yes my mountain flower and first I put my arms around him yes and drew him down to me so he could feel my breasts all perfume yes and his heart was going like mad and yes I said yes I will Yes

> —JAMES JOYCE,
> *Ulysses*, 1922

O, my luve's like a red red rose
That's newly sprung in June:
O my luve's like the melodie
That's sweetly played in tune.
> ━━ROBERT BURNS,
> *My Luve Is Like a Red Red Rose*, 1787

Love is a force. It is not a result; it is a cause. It is not a product; it produces. It is a power, like money or steam or electricity.
> ━━ANNE MORROW LINDBERGH,
> *Locked Rooms and Open Doors*, 1974

All mankind love a lover.
> ━━RALPH WALDO EMERSON,
> *Essays*, 1841

Love conquers all things; let us too surrender to Love.
> ━━VIRGIL,
> *Eclogues*

The first duty of love is to listen.
> ━━PAUL TILLICH,
> **recalled on his death, October 22, 1965**

He that loves a rosy cheek,
Or a coral lip admires,
Or, from star-like eyes, doth seek
Fuel to maintain his fires;
As old Time makes these decay,
So his flames must waste away.
> ━━THOMAS CAREW,
> **"Disdain Returned," 1640**

A woman happily in love, she burns the souffle. A woman unhappily in love, she forgets to turn on the oven.

→Baron St. Fontanel, in *Sabrina*,
    screenplay by ERNEST LEHMAN, BILLY WILDER, and SAMUEL
    TAYLOR, 1954

This as it will be seen is other far
Than with brooks taken otherwhere in song.
We love the things we love for what they are.

→ROBERT FROST,
    "Hyla Brook," 1916

How a little love and good company improves a woman!

→GEORGE FARQUHAR,
    The Beaux' Stratagem, 1707

We must love one another, yes, yes, that's all true enough, but nothing says we have to like each other.

→PETER DE VRIES,
    The Glory of the Hummingbird, 1974

Love begets love. This torment is my joy.

→THEODORE ROETHKE,
    The Motion, 1964

Now I adore my life
With the Bird, the abiding Leaf,
With the Fish, the questing Snail,
And the Eye altering all;
And I dance with William Blake
For love, for Love's sake.

→THEODORE ROETHKE,
    "Once More, The Round," 1964

Let those love now who never loved before;
Let those who always loved, now love the more.
  ━THOMAS PARNELL,
    translation of the *Pervigilium Veneris*, 1722

Come live with me, and be my love,
And we will some new pleasures prove
Of golden sands and crystal brooks
With silken lines, and silver hooks.
  ━JOHN DONNE,
    "The Bait," 1633

No, we don't accomplish our love in a single year as the flowers do;
an immemorial sap flows up through our arms when we love.
  ━RAINER MARIE RILKE,
    quoted *in The Selected Poetry of Rainer Maria Rilke,* translated
    by Stephen Mitchell, 1989

Dear love, for nothing less than thee
Would I have broke this happy dream,
It was a theme
For reason, much too strong for fantasy,
Therefore thou waked'st me wisely; yet
My dream thou brok'st not, but continued'st it.
  ━JOHN DONNE,
    The Dream, 1633

Love has the quality of informing almost everything—even one's
work.
  ━SYLVIA ASHTON-WARNER,
    Myself, 1967

How many loved your moments of glad grace,
And loved your beauty with love false or true,
But one man loved the pilgrim soul in you,
And loved the sorrows of your changing face
  ━WILLIAM BUTLER YEATS,
    "The Rose," 1893

I'm not a smart man, but I know what love is.

➤TOM HANKS as Forrest Gump,
Forrest Gump, 1994

The mind I love must have wild places, a tangled orchard where
dark damsons drop in the heavy grass, an overgrown little wood,
the chance of a snake or two, a pool that nobody's fathomed the
depth of, and paths threaded with flowers planted by the mind.

➤KATHERINE MANSFIELD,
Journal of Katherine Mansfield, 1927

If thou must love me, let it be for naught
Except for love's sake only.

➤ELIZABETH BARRETT BROWNING,
Sonnets from the Portuguese, 1850

Flower o' the broom,
Take away love, and our earth is a tomb!

➤ROBERT BROWNING,
Fra Lippo Lippi, 1855

On Waterloo Bridge I am trying to think:
This is nothing. You're high on the charm and the drink.
But the juke-box inside me is playing a song
that says something different. And when was it wrong?

➤WENDY COPE,
"After the Lunch," 1992

She loved me for the dangers I had passed,
And I loved her that she did pity them.

➤WILLIAM SHAKESPEARE,
Twelfth Night, 1601

I *am* Heathcliff—he's always, always in my mind—not as a pleasure, any more than I am always a pleasure to myself —but as my
own being.

➤Catherine Earnshaw in *Wuthering Heights*
by EMILY BRONTË, 1847

The fate of love is that it always seems too little or too much.
  ——AMELIA BARR,
    The Belle of Bowling Green, 1904

O lyric Love, half angel and half bird
And all a wonder and a wild desire.
  ——ROBERT BROWNING,
    The Ring and the Book, 1869

The world has little to bestow
Where two fond hearts in equal love are joined.
  ——ANNIE LAETITIA BARBAULD,
    "Delia," *The Works of Anna Laetitia Barbauld*, vol. 1, 1825

God is Love—I dare say. But what a mischievous devil Love is!
  ——SAMUEL BUTLER,
    "God Is Love," *Notebooks*, 1912

Alas! the love of women! it is known
To be a lovely and a fearful thing.
  ——LORD BYRON,
    Don Juan, 1818

We love because it's the only true adventure.
  ——NIKKI GIOVANNI,
    Reader's Digest, 1982

Only love interests me, and I am only in contact with things that
revolve around love.
  ——MARC CHAGALL,
    "Marc Chagall—Capturing the Exuberant Spirit," *Christian
    Science Monitor*, July 1, 1977

Love is not enough. It must be the foundation, the cornerstone, but
not the complete structure. It is much too pliable, too yielding.
  ——BETTE DAVIS,
    The Lonely Life, 1962

Oh! that the Desert were my dwelling-place,
With one fair Spirit for my minister,
That I might all forget the human race,
And, hating no one, love but only her!

— LORD BYRON,
Childe Harold's Pilgrimage, 1812

It was a love like a chord from Bach
of such pure gravity.

— NINA CASSIAN,
"It Was a Love," *Call Yourself Alive?*, 1988

We love as soon as we learn to distinguish a separate "you" and
"me." Love is our attempt to assuage the terror and isolation of that
separateness.

— JUDITH VIORST,
Necessary Losses, 1986

Love is patient, love is kind. It does not envy, it does not boast, it
is not proud. It is not rude, it is not self-seeking, it is not easily
angered, it keeps no record of wrongs. Love does not delight in
evil, but rejoices with the truth. It always protects, always trusts,
always hopes, always perseveres. Love never fails.

— 1 Corinthians 13:4-8

Love is a context, not a behavior.

— MARILYN FERGUSON,
The Aquarian Conspiracy, 1980

I love that you get cold when it's 71 degrees out. I love that it takes
you an hour and a half to order a sandwich. I love that you get a little crinkle in your nose when you're looking at me like I'm nuts. I
love that after I spend a day with you, I can still smell your perfume
on my clothes. And I love that you are the last person I want to talk
to before I go to sleep at night."

— Billy Crystal as Harry Burns, in *When Harry Met Sally*,
screenplay by NORA EPHRON, 1989

Love is a fruit in season all the time.

➤ MOTHER TERESA,
   A Gift for God, 1975

To say a man has fallen in love—or that he is deeply in love—or up
to the ears in love,—and sometimes even over head and ears in it—
carries an idiomatical kind of implication, that love is a thing
below a man.

➤ LAURENCE STERNE,
   Tristram Shandy, 1759

All love is sweet,
Given or returned. Common as light is love,
And its familiar voice wearies not ever.

➤ PERCY BYSSHE SHELLEY,
   Prometheus Unbound, 1819

Give all to love;
Obey thy heart; Friends, kindred, days,
Estate, good fame,
Plans, credit and the Muse,
Nothing refuse.

➤ RALPH WALDO EMERSON,
   "Give All to Love," 1847

Love is a spirit all compact of fire,
Not gross to sink, but light, and will aspire.

➤ WILLIAM SHAKESPEARE,
   Venus and Adonis, 1593

A pity beyond all telling,
Is hid in the heart of love.

➤ W. B. YEATS,
   "The Pity of Love," 1893

Love comforteth like sunshine after rain.

➤ WILLIAM SHAKESPEARE,
   Venus and Adonis, 1593

I wonder why love is so often equated with joy when it is everything else as well. Devastation, balm, obsession, granting and receiving excessive value, and losing it again. It is recognition, often of what you are not but might be. It scars and it heals, it is beyond pity and above law. It can seem like truth.

➤FLORIDA SCOT-MAXWELL,
The Measure of My Days, 1968

I thought love would adapt itself
to my needs.
But needs grow too fast;
they come up like weeds
Through cracks in the conversation.
Through silences in the dark.
Through everything you thought was concrete.

➤ALICE WALKER,
Did This Happen to Your Mother? Did Your Sister Throw Up a Lot?, 1979

Our deepest fear is not that we are inadequate. Our deepest fear is that we are powerful beyond measure. It is our light, not our darkness, that most frightens us.

➤MARIANNE WILLIAMSON,
A Return to Love, 1992

No cord nor cable can so forcibly draw, or hold so fast, as love can do with a twined thread.

➤ROBERT BURTON,
The Anatomy of Melancholy, 1621

Love Affairs

There is nothing better for the spirit or body than a love affair. It elevates thoughts and flattens stomachs.
➤ BARBARA HOWARD,
Laughing All the Way, 1973

Affairs, like revolutions, should only have beginnings.
➤ HOWARD SACKLER,
Goodbye Fidel, 1980

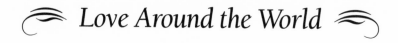

Love Around the World

A Canadian is somebody who knows how to make love in a canoe.
➤ PIERRE BERTON,
The Canadian, December 22, 1973

Do you know what "the English vice" really is? ...It's our refusal to admit our emotions. We think they demean us, I suppose.
➤ TERENCE RATTIGAN,
In Praise of Love, 1973

I was so cold I almost got married.
➤ SHELLEY WINTERS,
of England, *The New York Times*, April 25, 1956

France is the only place where you can make love in the afternoon without people hammering on your door.
➤ BARBARA CARTLAND,
Guardian, December 24, 1984

One becomes aware in France, after having lived in America, that sex pervades the air. It's there all around you, like a fluid.

    ➡HENRY MILLER,
        quoted in *Writers at Work* by George Plimpton, ed., 1963

It's true the French have a certain obsession with sex, but it's a particularly adult obsession. France is the thriftiest of all nations; to a Frenchman sex provides the most economical way to have fun. The French are a logical race.

    ➡ANITA LOOS,
        Kiss Hollywood Good-Bye, 1978

The isles of Greece, the isles of Greece!
Where burning Sappho loved and sung.

    ➡LORD BYRON,
        Don Juan, 1819

The Irish men are reckoned terrible heart stealers—but I do not find them so very formidable.

    ➡MARY WOLLSTONECRAFT,
        letter, May 11, 1787

Get yourself a Geisha. The flower of Asia,
She's one with whom to take up.
At night your bed she'll make up,
And she'll be there when you wake up.

    ➡HOWARD DIETZ,
        "Get Yourself a Geisha," 1935

Continental people have sex lives; the English have hot water bottles.

    ➡GEORGE MIKES,
        How to Be an Alien, 1946

The average Hollywood film star's ambition is to be admired by an American, courted by an Italian, married to an Englishman, and have a French boyfriend.

    ➡KATHARINE HEPBURN,
        New York Journal-American, February 22, 1954

 *Love at First Sight*

Who ever loved, that loved not at first sight?
━CHRISTOPHER MARLOWE,
Hero and Leander, 1598

O, there is nothing holier, in this life of ours, then the first consciousness of love, the first fluttering of its silken wings.
━HENRY WADSWORTH LONGFELLOW,
Hyperion, 1853

The advantage of love at first sight is that it delays a second sight.
━NATALIE CLIFFORD BARNEY,
"Adam," *Samples from Almost Illegible Notebooks*, 1962

(See also *Blind Love, Changeable Love, Enduring Love, Falling in Love, First Love, Foolish Love, Forbidden Love, Free Love, Great Love, Love, Loving, Mature Love, Memories of Love, True Love, Unrequited Love, Young Love*)

 *Love Letters*

Sir, more than kisses, letters mingle souls.
━JOHN DONNE,
"To Sir Henry Wotton," 1597

The very touch of the letter was as if you had taken me all into your arms.
━ANAIS NIN,
letter to Henry Miller, August 6, 1932

Our first love letter...the dread of saying too much is so nicely balanced by the fear of saying too little. Hope borders on presumption, and fear on reproach.

━L. E. LANDON,
Romance and Reality, 1831

Why it should be such an effort to write to the people one loves I can't imagine. It's none at all to write to those who didn't really count.

━KATHERINE MANSFIELD,
Journal of Katherine Mansfield, 1930

There's no finer caress than a love letter, because it makes the world very small, and the writer and reader, the only rulers.

━CECILIA CAPUZZI,
quoted in an article by Octavia Capuzzi Locke, *Johns Hopkins Magazine*, 1987

(See also *Communication, Enduring Love, Falling in Love, First Love, Foolish Love, Forbidden Love, Free Love, Love, Love at First Sight, Loving, Mature Love, Memories of Love, True Love, Unrequited Love, Young Love*)

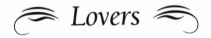

Lovers

In love, there is always one who kisses and one who offers the cheek.

━French proverb

A new commandment I give unto you, That ye love one another.

━St. John 13:34

No matter how much of a gargoyle someone is, if they are in love they have that spring in their step, accompanied by that infuriating I'm-in-an-exclusive-secret-special-club-and-you-don't-know-the password smugness.

> ⮞ARABELLA WEIR,
> *Does My Bum Look Big in This?*, 1997

The strongest influences in my life and my work are always whomever I love. Whomever I love and am with most of the time, or whomever I remember most vividly. I think that's true of everyone, don't you?

> ⮞TENNESSEE WILLIAMS,
> *The New York Times*, March 18, 1965

Him that I love, I wish to be free
Even from me

> ⮞ANNE MORROW LINDBERGH,
> "Even," *The Unicorn*, 1956

A lover's eyes will gaze an eagle blind;
A lover's ears will hear the lowest sound.

> ⮞WILLIAM SHAKESPEARE,
> *Love's Labours Lost*, 1595

It is something—it can be everything—to have found a fellow bird with whom you can sit among the rafters while the drinking and boasting and reciting and fighting go on below.

> ⮞WALLACE STEGNER,
> on finding a loved one,
> *The Spectator Bird*, 1976

It is easier to be a lover than a husband for the simple reason that it is more difficult to be witty every day than to say pretty things from time to time.

> ⮞HONORÉ DE BALZAC,
> *Physiologie du mariage*, 1829

Secretly, we wish that anyone we love will think exactly the way we do.
— KIM CHERNIN,
   In My Mother's House, 1983

We waste time looking for the perfect lover, instead of creating the perfect love.
— TOM ROBBINS,
   Still Life with Woodpecker, 1980

(See also *Blind Love, Changeable Love, Enduring Love, Falling in Love, First Love, Foolish Love, Forbidden love, Free Love, Great Love, Love, Love at First Sight, Loving, Mature Love, Memories of Love, True Love, Unrequited Love, Young Love*)

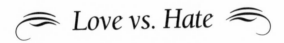

Love vs. Hate

Love lights more fires than hate extinguishes.
— ELLA WHEELER WILCOX,
   "Optimism," *Poems of Pleasure*, 1888

We fluctuate long between love and hatred before we can arrive at tranquility.
— HELOISE,
   first letter to Abelard, ca 1122

Were one merely to seek information, one should inquire of the man who hates, but if one wishes to know what truly is, one better ask the one who loves.
— HERMANN BROCH,
   The Spell, 1976

Hatred is a passion requiring one hundred times the energy of love. Keep it for a cause, not an individual.

—OLIVE MOORE,
Collected Writings, 1992

(See also *Enduring Love, Falling in Love, First Love, Foolish Love, Forbidden Love, Free Love, Love, Love at First Sight, Loving, Love vs. Like, Mature Love, Memories of Love, True Love, Unrequited Love, Young Love*)

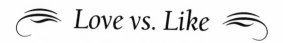 *Love vs. Like*

Love is like the wild rose-briar; Friendship like the holly-tree. The holly is dark when the rose-briar blooms, But which will bloom most constantly?

—EMILY BRONTË,
Love and Friendship, 1839

The end
of passion
may refashion
a friend

—MONA VAN DUYN,
"The Beginning," *Firefall*, 1993

Infinite hungers leap no more
In the chance swaying of your dress;
And love has changed to kindliness.

—RUPERT BROOKE,
"Kindliness," 1908

Love's the same as like except you feel sexier.

—JUDITH VIORST,
  Love and Guilt and the Meaning of Life, Etc., 1979

(See also *Changeable Love, Falling in Love, First Love, Foolish Love, Forbidden Love, Free Love, Love, Love at First Sight, Loving, Love vs. Hate, Mature Love, Memories of Love, True Love, Unrequited Love, Young Love*)

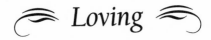

Loving

The story of a love is not important—what is important is that one is capable of love. It's perhaps the only glimpse we are permitted of eternity.

—HELEN HAYES,
  Guideposts, January 1960

The fate of love is that it always sees too little or too much.

—AMELIA E. BARR,
  The Belle of Bowling Green, 1904

To love and be loved is to feel the sun from both sides.

—DAVID VISCOTT,
  How to Live with Another Person, 1974

I have drunk of the wine of life at last, I have known the thing best worth knowing, I have been warmed through and through, never to grow quite cold again til the end.

—EDITH WHARTON,
  quoted in *The Sexual Education of Edith Wharton* by Gloria C. Erlich, 1992

There is no surprise more magical than the surprise of being loved:
It is God's finger on man's shoulder.
> ⟵CHARLES MORGAN,
> recalled on his death, February 6, 1968

Accustom yourself continually to make many acts of love, for they
enkindle and melt the soul.
> ⟵ST. TERESA OF AVILA,
> "Maxims for Her Nuns," quoted in *Selected Writings of St.
> Teresa of Avila* by E. Allison Peers and William J. Doheny,
> eds., 1950

I have no patience with women who measure and weigh their love
like a country doctor dispensing capsules. If a man is worth loving
at all, he is worth loving generously, even recklessly.
> ⟵MARIE DRESSLER,
> *The Life Story of an Ugly Duckling*, 1924

The daughter had come to meet me
When her parents tried to prevent it.
I spoke soft words to her.
She did not answer.
You will grow old there, you and remorse:
We and love
Shall go home to our house.
> ⟵JEAN-JOSEPH RABEARIVELO,
> *Old Songs of Imerina Land*, 1939

Each one of us thinks our experience of love is different from
everybody else's.
> ⟵VIBHAVARI SHIRURKAR,
> quoted in *Women Writing in India* by Susie Tharu and
> K. Lalita, eds., 1991

(See also *Enduring Love, Falling in Love, First Love, Foolish Love,
Forbidden Love, Free Love, Love, Love at First Sight, Love vs. Hate,
Love vs. Like, Mature Love, Memories of Love, True Love, Unrequited
Love, Young Love*)

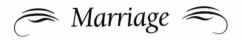

Marriage

One advantage of marriage, it seems to me, is that when you fall out of love with him, or he falls out of love with you, it keeps you together until you maybe fall in again.

—JUDITH VIORST,
"What Is This Thing Called Love?" *Redbook*, February 1975

I would say that the surest measure of a man's or a woman's maturity is the harmony, style, joy, and dignity he creates in his marriage, and the pleasure and inspiration he provides for his spouse.

—BENJAMIN SPOCK,
quoted in *Older & Wiser: 716 Memorable Quotes from Those Who Have Lived the Longest and Seen the Most* by G. B. Dianda and B. J. Hofmayer, eds., 1995

Every marriage is a battle between two families struggling to reproduce themselves.

—CARL WHITAKER,
The New York Times, April 25, 1995

I would like to have engraved inside every wedding band *Be kind to one another*. This is the Golden Rule of marriage and the secret of making love last through the years.

—RANDOLPH RAY,
My Little Church around the Corner, 1957

Marriage should always combat the monster that devours everything: habit.

—HONORÉ DE BALZAC,
Physiology of Marriage, 1829

Marriage is a series of desperate arguments people feel passionately about.

—KATHARINE HEPBURN,
Kate, 1975

It doesn't much signify whom one marries, for one is sure to find next morning that it was someone else.

➤ SAMUEL ROGERS,
    quoted in *Table Talk of Samuel Rogers* by Alexander Dyce, ed., 1890

Marriage is a feast where the grace is sometimes better than the dinner.

➤ CHARLES CALEB COLTON,
    Lacon, 1822

A successful marriage requires falling in love many times, always with the same person.

➤ MIGNON MCLAUGHLIN,
    The Second Neurotic's Notebook, 1966

Take each other for better or worse, but not for granted.

➤ ARLENE DAHL,
    Always Ask a Man, 1965

Marriage is a wonderful invention; but then again, so is a bicycle repair kit.

➤ BILLY CONNOLLY,
    quoted in *Billy Connolly* by Duncan Campbell, 1976

When a woman gets married it is like jumping into a hole in the ice in the middle of winter; you do it once and you remember it the rest of your days.

➤ MAXIM GORKY,
    The Lower Depths, 1903

It takes a long time to be really married. One marries many times at many levels within a marriage. If you have more marriages than you have divorces within the marriage, you're lucky and you stick it out.

➤ RUBY DEE,
    quoted in *I Dream a World* by Brian Lanker, 1989

Never marry a man who hates his mother, because he'll end up hating you.

—JILL BENNETT,
Observer, September 12, 1982

The married ones are those who have taken the terrible risk of intimacy and having taken it, know life without intimacy to be impossible.

—CAROLYN HEILBRUN,
Ms., August 1974

Look for a sweet person. Forget rich.

—ESTÉE LAUDER,
advice on choosing a spouse, *The New Yorker*, September 15, 1986

My love for you is mixed throughout my body.

—ANONYMOUS,
Love Songs of the New Kingdom, 1550–1080 B.C.

People stay married because they want to, not because the doors are locked.

—PAUL NEWMAN,
Winning, 1969

No one on this planet ever really chooses each other. I mean, it's all a question of quantum physics, molecular attraction and timing.

—RON SHELTON,
Bull Durham, 1988

So they were married—to be the more together—
And found they were never again so much together,
Divided by the morning tea,
By the evening paper,
By children and tradesmen's bills.

—LOUIS MACNEICE,
"Les Sylphides," 1941

Staying married may have long-term benefits. You can elicit much more sympathy from friends over a bad marriage than you ever can from a good divorce.

➤ P. J. O'ROURKE,
Modern Manners, 1984

Marriage is like a besieged castle; those who are on the outside wish to get in; and those who are on the inside wish to get out.

➤ Arabian Proverb

Love is not weakness. It is strong. Only the sacrament of marriage can contain it.

➤ BORIS PASTERNAK,
Dr. Zhivago, 1958

There is probably nothing like living together for blinding people to each other.

➤ IVY COMPTON-BURNETT,
quoted in *Uncommon Scold* by Abby Adams, 1989.

Like everyone who is not in love, he imagined that one chose the person whom one loved after endless deliberations and on the strength of various qualities and advantages.

➤ MARCEL PROUST,
Cities of the Plain, 1922

Marriage is our last, best chance to grow up.

➤ JOSEPH BARTH,
Ladies Home Journal, April 1961

Let me not to the marriage of true minds
Admit impediments. Love is not love
Which alters when it alteration finds
Or bends with the remover to remove.
O, no! it is an ever-fix'd mark
That looks on tempests and is never shaken.

➤ WILLIAM SHAKESPEARE,
Sonnet XVI, ca 1598

To keep your marriage brimming
With love in the loving cup,
Whenever you're wrong, admit it;
Whenever you're right, shut up.

➤ OGDEN NASH,
Marriage Lines, 1964

Where one goes wrong when looking for the ideal girl is in making one's selection before walking the full length of the counter.

➤ P. G. WODEHOUSE,
Much Obliged, Jeeves, 1971

In my father's day a man married the first woman who allowed him to unclasp her brassiere. And a woman married the first man she met who had a job and didn't wipe his nose on his suit coat sleeve.

➤ P. J. O'ROURKE,
Age and Guile, 1995

Hail wedded love, mysterious law, true source
Of human offspring, sole propriety
In Paradise of all things common else.

➤ JOHN MILTON,
Paradise Lost, 1667

Daisy, Daisy, give me your answer, do!
I'm half crazy, all for the love of you!
It won't be a stylish marriage,
I can't afford a carriage,
But you'll look sweet upon the seat
Of a bicycle built for two!

➤ HARRY DACRE,
Daisy Bell, 1892

Marriage is popular because it combines the maximum of temptations with the maximum of opportunity.

➤ GEORGE BERNARD SHAW,
The Devil's Disciple, 1901

Constant togetherness is fine—but only for Siamese twins.

   —VICTORIA BILLINGS,
     The Womansbook, 1974

Where there's Marriage without Love, there will be Love without Marriage.

   —BENJAMIN FRANKLIN,
     Poor Richard's Almanac, 1734

Perhaps loving something is the only starting place there is for making your life your own.

   —ALICE KOLLER,
     An Unknown Woman, 1982

The deep, deep peace of the double-bed after the hurly-burly of the chaise lounge.

   —MRS. PATRICK CAMPBELL,
     While Rome Burns, 1934

Love and marriage, love and marriage,
Go together like a horse and carriage.

   —SAMMY CAHN,
     Our Town, 1955

For I'm not so old and not so plain,
And I'm quite prepared to marry again.

   —SIR WILLIAM S. GILBERT,
     Iolanthe, 1882

There's nothing so nice as a new marriage. No psychoses yet, no aggressions, no guilt complexes.

   —BEN HECHT,
     Spellbound, 1945

The sum which two married people owe to one another defies calculation. It is an infinite debt, which can only be discharged through all eternity.

—JOHANN WOLFGANG VON GOETHE,
Elective Affinities, 1808

Perhaps this is in the end what most marriages are—gentleness, memory and habit.

—STORM JAMESON,
That Was Yesterday, 1932

For what is wedlock forced, but a hell,
An age of discord and continual strife?
Whereas the contrary bringeth bliss,
And is a pattern of celestial peace.

—WILLIAM SHAKESPEARE,
King Henry VI, 1591

I suspect that in every good marriage there are times when love seems to be over.

—MADELEINE L'ENGLE,
Two-Part Invention, 1988

To keep the fire burning brightly there's one easy rule: Keep the two logs together, near enough to keep each other warm and far enough apart—about a finger's breadth—for breathing room. Good fire, good marriage, same rule.

—MARNIE REED CROWELL,
Greener Pastures, 1973

He has married me with a ring, a ring of bright water
Whose ripples spread from the heart of the sea,
He has married me with a ring of light, the glitter
Broadcast on the swift river.

—KATHLEEN RAINE,
The Marriage of Psyche, 1952

I know I weigh seventeen stone and my missus looks like a ninepenny rabbit, and yet we're as happy as can be.
　　—P. G. WODEHOUSE,
　　　Summer Lightning, 1929

(See also Enduring Love, Falling in Love, Honeymoon, Husbands, In-Laws, Love, Loving, Mature Love, Memories of Love, True Love, Wives, Young Love)

Mature Love

Love's like the measles—all the worse when it comes late in life.
　　—DOUGLAS JERROLD,
　　　"A Philanthropist," Wit and Opinions, 1859

When I look back on the pain of sex, the love like a wild fox so ready to bite, the antagonism that sits like a twin beside love, and contrast it with affection, so deeply unrepeatable, of two people who have lived a life together (and of whom one must die), it's the affection I find richer. It's that I would have again. Not all those doubtful rainbow colours.
　　—ENID BAGNOLD,
　　　Autobiography, 1974

They are in love, they have always been in love, although sometimes they would have denied it. And because they have been in love they have survived everything that life could throw at them, even their own failures.
　　—ERNEST HAVEMANN,
　　　on a long-married couple, "Love and Marriage," Life, September 29, 1961

Summer days are over!
O my one true lover
Sit we now alone together
In the early autumn weather!
From our nest the birds have flown
To fair dreamlands of their own
And we see the days go by
In silence—thou and I!
> ◄—JULIA C. R. DORR,
> "Thou and I," *Poems*, 1892

You see I thought love got easier over the years so it didn't hurt so bad when it hurt, or feel so good when it felt good. I thought it smoothed out and old people hardly noticed it. I thought it curled up and died, I guess. Now I saw it rear up like a whip and lash.
> ◄—LOUISE ERDICH,
> *Love Machine*, 1984

One of those looks which only a quarter-century of wedlock can adequately marinate.
> ◄—ALAN COREN,
> *Seems Like Old Times*, 1989

A man is often too young to marry, but a man is never too old to love.
> ◄—Old Finnish proverb

Immature love says: "I love you because I need you."
Mature love says: "I need you because I love you."
> ◄—Confucious proverb

When you are very old, and sit in the candlelight at evening sitting by the fire, you will say, as you murmur my verses, a wonder in your eyes, "Ronsard sang of me in the days when I was fair."
> ◄—PIERRE DE RONSARD,
> *Sonnets pour Helene*, 1578

I shall grow skinnier as you grow paunched, a Laurel to your Hardy.

⬤—ELAINE FEINSTEIN,
Valentine for a Middle-Aged Spouse, 1990

May-December Romance

How absurd and delicious it is to be in love with somebody younger than yourself! Everybody should try it.

⬤—BARBARA PYM,
quoted in *A Lot to Ask* by Hazel Holt, 1990

He was rich and old and she
Was thirty-two or thirty-three.
She gave him fifteen years to life—
the only thing she meant to give.

⬤—JUSTIN RICHARDSON,
"Wholly Matrimony," 1949

(See also *Age, Enduring Love, Falling in Love, Foolish Love, Forbidden Love, Free Love, Love, Loving, Mature Love, Memories of Love, True Love, Unrequited Love*)

Memories of Love

He who truly loves never forgets.

⬤—Mexican proverb

There should be an invention that bottles up a memory like a perfume, and it never faded, never got stale, and whenever I wanted to I could uncork the bottle, and live the memory all over again.

➤ DAPHNE DU MAURIER,
Rebecca, 1938

The memories of long love gather like drifting snow, poignant as the mandarin ducks who float side by side in sleep.

➤ LADY MURASAKI,
The Tale of Genji, ca 1008

Remember me when I am gone away,
Gone far away into the silent land;
When you can no more hold me by the hand,
Nor I half turn to go yet turning stay.

➤ CHRISTINA ROSSETTI,
"Remember," 1862

Rose leaves, when the rose is dead,
Are heaped for the beloved's bed;
And so thy thoughts, when thou art gone,
Love itself shall slumber on.

➤ PERCY BYSSHE SHELLEY,
"Music When Soft Voices Die," 1824

Love makes up for the lack of long memories by a sort of magic. All other affections need a past; love creates a past which envelopes us, as if by enchantment.

➤ BENJAMIN CONSTANT,
Adolphe, 1816

And the best and the worst of this is
That neither is most to blame,
If you have forgotten my kisses
And I have forgotten your name.

➤ ALGERNON CHARLES SWINBURNE,
"An Interlude," 1866

When the lamp is shattered,
The light in the dust lies dead—
When the cloud is scattered
The rainbow's glory is shed.
When the lute is broken,
Sweet tones are remembered not;
When the lips have spoken,
Loved accents are soon forgot.

    ━PERCY BYSSHE SHELLEY,
       "Lines," 1824

Memory is to love what the saucer is to the cup.

    ━ELIZABETH BOWEN,
       The House in Paris, 1935

I have forgot much, Cynara! gone with the wind,
Flung roses, roses, riotously, with the throng,
Dancing, to put thy pale, lost lilies out of mind.

    ━ERNEST DOWSON,
       "Non sum Qualis Eram," 1896

Haply I think on thee,—and then my state,
Like to the lark at break of day arising
From sullen earth, sings hymns at heaven's gate;
For thy sweet love remembered such wealth brings
That then I scorn to change my state with kings.

    ━WILLIAM SHAKESPEARE,
       Sonnet 29, c 1598

(See also *Enduring Love, Falling in Love, First Love, Foolish Love, Forbidden Love, Free Love, Love, Love at First Sight, Loving, True Love, Unrequited Love, Young Love*)

Men

The man who treasures his friends is usually solid gold himself.

━━MARJORIE HOLMES,
Love and Laughter, 1967

Love is like playing checkers. You have to know which man to move.

━━JACKIE "MOMS" MABLEY,
interview in *Black Stars*, May 1973

I love men, not because they are men, but because they are not women.

━━CHRISTINA OF SWEDEN,
"Maxims, 1660–1680," *Pensées de Christine, Reine de Suede*,
1825

Can you imagine a world without men? No crime and lots of fat, happy women.

━━NICOLE HOLLANDER,
Sylvia, 1981

Do you know why God withheld the sense of humour from women?
That we may love you instead of laughing at you.

━━MRS. PATRICK CAMPBELL,
"To a Man," quoted in *The Life of Mrs. Pat* by M. Peters, 1940

You have to be very fond of men. Very, very fond. You have to be very fond of them to love them. Otherwise, they're simply unbearable.

━━MARGUERITE DURAS,
Practicalities, 1987

It's not the men in my life that counts, it's the life in my men.

    ➤MAE WEST,
      Diamond Lil, 1932

Immodest creature, you do not want a woman who will accept your faults, you want one who pretends that you are faultless—one who will caress the hand that strikes her and kiss the lips that lie to her.

    ➤GEORGE SAND,
      Intimate Journal, 1926

Bloody men are like bloody buses—
You wait for about a year
And as soon as one approaches your stop
Two or three others appear.

    ➤WENDY COPE,
      "Bloody Men," 1992

It was the promise of men, that around each corner there was yet another man, more wonderful than the last, that sustained me. You see, I had men confused with life… You can't get what I wanted from a man, not in this life.

    ➤NANCY FRIDAY,
      My Mother, My Self, 1977

 *Money*

Love is not to be bought, in any sense of the word; its silken wings are instantly shrivelled up when any thing beside a return in kind is sought.

    ➤MARY WOLLSTONECRAFT,
      A Vindication of the Rights of Woman, 1792

For money has a power above
The stars and fate, to manage love.
— SAMUEL BUTLER,
Hudibras, part 3, 1680

And all for love, and nothing for reward.
— EDMUND SPENSER,
The Faerie Queen, 1596

 Music

Give me some music—music, moody food
Of us that trade in love.
— WILLIAM SHAKESPEARE,
Antony and Cleopatra, 1606

If music be the food of love, play on;
Give me excess of it, that, surfeiting,
The appetite may sicken, and so die.
— WILLIAM SHAKESPEARE,
Twelfth Night, 1601

The man who is not thrilled to the bone by the sight of a woman
playing the flute, blowing a clarinet or struggling with the intrica-
cies of a trombone is no man.
— MALCOLM SARGENT,
quoted in *Peacocks on the Podium* by Charles Gattey, 1982

Maybe the most that you can expect from a relationship that goes
bad is to come out of it with a few good songs.
— MARIANNE FAITHFULL,
Faithfull, 1994

All my life I was having trouble with women...Then, after I quit having trouble with them, I could feel in my heart that somebody would always have trouble with them, so I keep writing those blues.

—MUDDY WATERS,
 quoted in *All You Need Is Love* by Tony Palmer, 1976

I conclude that musical notes and rhythms were first acquired by the male or female progenitors of mankind for the sake of charming the opposite sex.

—CHARLES DARWIN,
 The Descent of Man, 1871

"Bed," as the Italian proverb succinctly puts it, "is the poor man's opera."

—ALDOUS HUXLEY,
 Heaven and Hell, 1956

Consort not with a female musician lest thou be taken in by her snares.

—BEN SIRA,
 The Book of Wisdom, ca 190 B.C.

(See also *Enduring Love, Falling in Love, First Love, Foolish Love, Forbidden Love, Free Love, Love, Love at First Sight, Loving, Memories of Love, True Love, Unrequited Love, Young Love*)

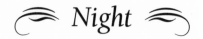

Night

For the night
Shows stars and women in a better light.

—LORD BYRON,
 Don Juan, 1819

Give me my Romeo: and, when he shall die,
Take him and cut him out in little stars,
And he will make the face of heaven so fine
That all the world will be in love with night,
And pay no worship to the garish sun.

    ━WILLIAM SHAKESPEARE,
       Romeo and Juliet, 1595

Three matches in the night lit one by one.
The first to see your whole face.
The second to see your eyes.
The last to see your mouth.
And then deep darkness to let me remember it all.
As I hold you in my arms.

    ━JACQUES PREVERT,
       "Paris at Night," 1949

On the Rebound ...

Transplanted love rarely prospers.

    ━**Indian proverb**

All discarded lovers should be given a second chance, but with
somebody else.

    ━MAE WEST,
       **quoted in *The Wit and Wisdom of Mae West* by Joseph Wein-
        traub, ed., 1967**

(See also *Betrayal, End of Love, Divorce, Falling in Love, First Love,
Foolish Love, Forbidden Love, Love, Loving, Young Love*)

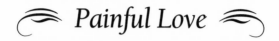

Painful Love

Mortal love is but the licking of honey from thorns.
—Anonymous woman at the court of Eleanor of Aquitaine,
in *Whistling Girl* by Helen Lawrenson, 1978

Pains of love be sweeter far
Than all other pleasures are.
—JOHN DRYDEN,
"Tyrannic Love," 1669

I have found the paradox that if I love until it hurts, then there is
no hurt, but only more love.
—DAPHNE RAE,
Love Until It Hurts, 1980

The pain of love is the pain of being alive. It's a perpetual wound.
—MAUREEN DUFFY,
Wounds, 1969

I am not sure at all
if love is salve
or just
a deeper kind of wound
I do not think it matters
—ERICA JONG,
"The Evidence," *Half-Lives*, 1971

(See also *End of Love, Divorce, Falling in Love, First Love, Foolish
Love, Forbidden Love, Hard to Get, Heartbreak, Loneliness, Love,
Unrequited Love, Young Love*)

Parting

To part is to die a little;
To die to what we love.
We leave behind a bit of ourselves
Wherever we have been.

➤ EDMOND HARAUCOURT,
Choix de Poesies, Rondel de l'Adieu, 1891

If I can let you go as trees let go
...Lose what I lose to keep what I can keep,
The strong root still alive under the snow,
Love will endure—if I can let you go.

➤ MAY SARTON,
"The Autumn Sonnets," *A Durable Fire*, 1972

It is never any good dwelling on goodbyes. It is not the being
together that it prolongs but the parting.

➤ ELIZABETH BIBESCO,
The Fir and the Palm, 1924

The boy's woe was as keen and clear
The boy's love just as true
And the One before Last, my dear,
Hurt quite as much as you.

➤ RUPERT BROOKE,
"The One Before Last," 1908

O Where are you going? stay with me here!
Were the vows you swore me deceiving, deceiving?
No, I promised to love you, dear,
But I must be leaving.

➤ W. H. AUDEN,
"O What Is that Sound Which So Thrills the Ear?" 1936

Leaving can sometimes be the best way to never go away.
— CATHY N. DAVIDSON,
36 Views of Mount Fuji, 1993

Good night, good night!
parting is such sweet sorrow,
That I shall say good night
till it be morrow.
— WILLIAM SHAKESPEARE,
Romeo and Juliet, 1596

Say what you will, 'tis better to be left than never to have been
loved.
— WILLIAM CONGREVE,
The Way of the World, 1700

Woman much missed, how you call to me, call to me.
Saying that now you are not as you were
When you had changed from the one who was all to me,
But as at first, when our day was fair.
— THOMAS HARDY,
The Voice, 1914

In every parting there is the image of death.
— GEORGE ELIOT,
Scenes of Clerical Life, 1858

He was my North, my South, my East and West,
My working week and my Sunday rest,
My noon, my midnight, my talk, my song;
I thought that love would last forever: I was wrong.
— W. H. AUDEN,
"Funeral Blues," 1936

Farewell! Thou art too dear for my possessing.
— WILLIAM SHAKESPEARE,
Sonnet 87, 1603–1604

Somehow, the real moment of parting always precedes the physical act of separation.

> ← Princess Marthe Bibesco,
> *Catherine-Paris*, 1928

Silently and hopelessly I loved you,
At times too jealous and at times too shy.
God grant you find another who will love you
As tenderly and truthfully as I.

> ← Alexander Pushkin,
> "I Loved You," 1829

A man never knows how to say goodbye; a woman never knows when to say it.

> ← Helen Rowland,
> *Reflections of a Bachelor Girl*, 1903

I remember the way we parted,
The day and the way we met;
You hoped we were both broken-hearted,
And knew we should both forget.

> ← Algernon Charles Swinburne,
> "An Interlude," 1886

How can I live without thee, how forgo
Thy sweet converse and love so dearly joined,
To live again in these wild woods forlorn?

> ← John Milton,
> *Paradise Lost*, 1667

Our parting now will dampen
Rumours we have not denied.
This gown will rot away
From tears of intense longing.

> ← Lady Nijo,
> letter to Iinuma, 1289

There's no love song finer,
But how strange the change from major to minor
Every time we say goodbye.
    ➳COLE PORTER,
        "Every Time We Say Goodbye," 1944

You and I, when our days are done, must say
Without exactly saying it, goodbye.
    ➳JOHN FULLER,
        "Pyrosymphonnie," 1996

(See also *Betrayal, Death, Divorce, End of Love, Farewell, Forbidden Love, Heartbreak, Painful Love*)

Passion

The only difference between a caprice and a lifelong passion is that the caprice lasts a little longer.
    ➳OSCAR WILDE,
        The Picture of Dorian Gray, 1891

In her first passion woman loves her lover,
In all the others, all she loves is love.
    ➳LORD BYRON,
        Don Juan, 1819

Wild Nights—Wild Nights
Were I with thee
Wild Nights should be
Our luxury!
    ➳EMILY DICKINSON,
        quoted in *Poems by Emily Dickinson* by T. W. Higginson and
        Mabel Loomis Todd, eds., 1891

How little do they know human nature, who think they can say to passion, so far shalt thou go, and no farther!

➤SARAH SCOTT,
The History of Cornelia, 1750

Let men tremble to win the hand of woman, unless they win along with it the utmost passion of her heart.

➤NATHANIEL HAWTHORNE,
The Scarlet Letter, 1850

Great passions, my dear, don't exist; they're liars' fantasies. What do exist are little loves that may last for a short or a longer while.

➤ANNA MAGNANI,
quoted in *Limelighters* by Orianna Fallaci, 1963

Experience teaches us in a millennium what passion teaches us in an hour.

➤RALPH IRON,
The Story of an African Farm, 1883

There's plenty of fire in the coldest flint!

➤RACHEL FIELD,
All This and Heaven Too! 1939

A continual atmosphere of hectic passion is very trying if you haven't got any of your own.

➤DOROTHY L. SAYERS,
The Unpleasantness at the Bellona Club, 1928

One mad magenta moment and I have paid for it all my life.

➤ALAN BENNETT,
Habeas Corpus, 1973

How little of permanent happiness could belong to a couple who were only brought together because their passions were stronger than their virtue.

➤JANE AUSTEN,
Pride and Prejudice, 1813

To me, passionate love has always been like a tight shoe rubbing blisters on my Achilles heel... I resent it and love it and wallow and recover...and I wish to God I could handle it, but I never have and I know I never will.

➤ NOEL COWARD,
    Diary, December 1, 1957

A man who has not passed through the inferno of his passions has never overcome them.

➤ CARL G. JUNG,
    Memories, Dreams, Reflections, 1962

Passion should believe itself irresistible. It should forget civility and consideration and all the other curses of a refined nature. Above all, it should never ask for leave where there is a right of way.

➤ E. M. FORSTER,
    A Room with a View, 1908

Passion makes the world go round. Love just makes it a safer place.

➤ ICE-T,
    The Ice Opinion, 1994

(See also *Desire, Enduring Love, Falling in Love, First Love, Free Love, Love, Loving, Mature Love, Memories of Love, Seduction, True Love, Young Love*)

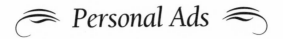

Personal Ads

What everyone's groping for, through the artificial mists, is harder to put into an ad; the touch of kindred, the shared current of light.
— BARBARA HOLLAND,
One's Company, 1992

(See also *Courtship*)

Pleasure

If I had no duties, and no reference to futurity, I would spend my life in driving briskly in a post-chaise with a pretty woman.
— SAMUEL JOHNSON,
quoted in *Life of Johnson* by James Boswell, 1791

In love, as in gluttony, pleasure is a matter of the utmost precision.
— ITALO CALVINO,
quoted in *Theory of the Four Movements* by Charles Fourier, 1971

Time is short, and we must seize
Those pleasures found above the knees
— RICHARD EYRE,
Utopia and Other Places, 1993

The pleasure of love is loving, and we get more happiness from the passion we feel than from the passion we inspire.
— DUC DE LA ROCHEFOUCAULD,
Maximes, 1678

Let us have wine and women, mirth and laughter,
Sermons and soda-water the day after.
━LORD BYRON,
Don Juan, 1819

(See also *Desire, Passion*)

Poets

I suspect
There would be more poems
About sex
If it rhymed with more than
Pecks
Necks
Erects and ejects.
━LYNN PETERS,
quoted in *Making Love to Marilyn* by Susan Robert, ed., 1998

Chameleons feed on light and air.
Poets' food is love and fame
━PERCY BYSSHE SHELLEY,
"An Exhortation," 1819

The lunatic, the lover and the poet
Are of imagination all compact.
━WILLIAM SHAKESPEARE,
A Midsummer Night's Dream, 1596

A poet without love were a physical and metaphysical impossibility.
━THOMAS CARLYLE,
Edinburgh Review, 1928

I was only a poor poet, made for singing at her casement,
As the finches or the thrushes, while she thought of other things.

> ←ELIZABETH BARRETT BROWNING,
> *Lady Geraldine's Courtship*, 1844

I used to think all poets were Byronnic.
They're mostly wicked as a ginless tonic
And wild as pension plans.

> ←WENDY COPE,
> "Triolet," 1986

I court others in verse: but I love thee in prose:
And they have my whimsies, but thou hast my heart.

> ←MATTHEW PRIOR,
> *A Better Answer*, 1718

Wherever you've got to in the tunnel of love, remember that some
poet has been there before you.

> ←DAISY GOODWIN,
> introduction to *The Nation's Favourite Love Poems*, 1997

When amatory poets sing their loves
In liquid lines mellifluously bland,
And pair their rhymes as Venus yokes her doves,
They little think what mischief is in hand.

> ←LORD BYRON,
> *Don Juan*, 1819

 *Poverty*

But I, being poor, have only my dreams;
I have spread my dreams under your feet;
Tread softly because you tread on my dreams.
　—W. B. YEATS,
　　"He Wishes for the Cloths of Heaven," 1899

Here men say a comyn proverbe in englond that love lastest as
longe as the money endurith
　—CAXTON,
　　Game of Chess, 1474

(See also *Money*)

 *Problems*

It's odd that you can get so anesthetized by your own pain or your
own problem that you don't quite fully share the hell of someone
close to you.
　—LADY BIRD JOHNSON,
　　A White House Diary, 1970

She did observe, with some dismay, that far from conquering all,
love lazily sidestepped practical problems.
　—JEAN STAFFORD,
　　"The Liberation," *The Collected Stories of Jean Stafford,* 1969

Love laughs at locksmiths.
　—GEORGE COLMAN, the Younger,
　　Love Laughs at Locksmiths, 1808

Make sure you never, never argue at night. You just lose a good night's sleep and you can't settle anything until morning anyway.

⬩ ROSE KENNEDY,
    advice to her first married granddaughter,
    People, January 6, 1983

 *Promises*

But what a woman says to her lusting lover it is best to write in wind and swift-flowing water.

⬩ CATULLUS,
    Carmina, ca 84–54 B.C.

By the time you say you're his,
Shivering and sighing
And he vows his passion is
Infinite, undying—
Lady, make a note of this:
One of you is lying.

⬩ DOROTHY PARKER,
    "Unfortunate Coincidence," 1937

O! Swear not by the moon, the inconstant moon,
That monthly changes in her circled orb,
Lest that thy love prove likewise variable.

⬩ WILLIAM SHAKESPEARE,
    Romeo and Juliet, 1595

 *Proposals*

Once a week is quite enough to propose to anyone, and it should always be done in a manner that attracts some attention.

—OSCAR WILDE,
An Ideal Husband, 1895

I'm afraid I was very much the traditionalist. I went down on one knee and dictated a proposal which my secretary faxed over straight away.

—STEPHEN FRY and HUGH LAURIE,
A Bit More Fry and Laurie, 1991

Use any form of proposal you like. Try to avoid abstract nouns.

—JOE ORTON,
Loot, 1967

He also reminded her that she was at a time of life when she could hardly expect to pick and choose, and that her spiritual condition was one of, at least, great uncertainty. These combined statements are held, under the law of Scotland at any rate, to be equivalent to an offer of marriage.

—STEPHEN LEACOCK,
Arcadian Adventures with the Idle Rich, 1914

(See also *Marriage*)

 # *Regret*

Never regret. If it's good, it's wonderful. If it's bad, it's experience.

— VICTORIA HOLT,
The Black Opal, 1993

Love lives in sealed bottles of regret.

— SEAN O'FAOLAIN,
"The Jungle of Love," *Saturday Evening Post*, August 13, 1966

Non! rien de rien,
Non! Je ne regrette rien,
Ni le bien, qu'on m'a fait,
Ni le mal—tout ca m'est bien egal!
No, no regrets,
No, we will have no regrets,
As you leave, I can say—

— MICHEL VAUCAIRE:
"Non, je ne regrette rien," song sung by Edith Piaf, 1960

There can be no deep disappointment where there is not deep love.

— MARTIN LUTHER KING, JR.,
"Letter from Birmingham Jail," *Why We Can't Wait*, 1963

There is perhaps no surer mark of folly, than to attempt to correct natural infirmities of those we love.

— HENRY FIELDING,
Tom Jones, 1749

Then, must you speak
Of one that loved not wisely but too well.

— WILLIAM SHAKESPEARE,
Othello, 1602

Had I said that, had I done this,
So might I gain, so might I miss. Might she have loved me? Just as well
She might have hated, who can tell!
— ROBERT BROWNING,
The Last Ride Together, 1855

To think that I've wasted years of my life, that I've longed to die, that I've experienced my greatest love for a woman who didn't appeal to me, who wasn't even my type!
— MARCEL PROUST,
Swann's Way, 1913

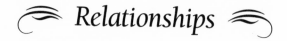 *Relationships*

A relationship isn't meant to be an insurance policy, a life preserver or a security blanket.
— DIANE CROWLEY,
Column, 1992

We cannot have an identity all alone. Our reality is shaped from the beginning by a relationship.
— JOHN BRADSHAW,
quoted in *One's Company* by Barbara Holland, 1992

If one is out of touch with oneself, then one cannot touch others.
— ANNE MORROW LINDBERGH,
Gifts from the Sea, 1955

Kindness and intelligence don't always deliver us from the pitfalls and traps: there are always failures of love, of will, of imagination. There is no way to take the danger out of human relationships.
— BARBARA GRIZZUTI HARRISON,
"Secrets Women Tell Each Other," *McCall's*, August 1975

Now the whole dizzying and delirious range of sexual possibilities has been boiled down to that one big, boring, bulimic word: Relationship.
— JULIE BURCHILL,
"The Dead Zone," *Arena*, 1988

We want to be part of a couple. Uncoupled, we are all slightly diminished in sheer bulk...there's a danger in certain moods and at certain times of year, of simply blowing off the face of the world like a scrap of crumbled paper.
— BARBARA HOLLAND,
One's Company, 1992

In the beginning of all relationships you are out there bungee jumping every weekend but after six months you are renting videos and buying corn chips just like everyone else—and the next day you can't even remember what video you rented.
— DOUGLAS COUPLAND,
Life After God, 1994

(See also *Enduring Love, Falling in Love, First Love, Foolish Love, Forbidden Love, Free Love, Love, Loving, Love vs. Hate, Love vs. Like, Mature Love, Memories of Love, True Love, Unrequited Love, Young Love*)

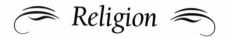

Religion

There is no religion without love, and people may talk as much as they like about their religion, but if it does not teach them to be good and kind to man and beast, it is all a sham.

— ANNA SEWELL,
Black Beauty, 1877

The one certain way for a woman to hold a man is to leave him for religion.

— DAME MURIEL SARAH SPARK,
The Comforters, 1957

Religion is love; in no case is it logic.

— BEATRICE POTTER WEBB,
My Apprenticeship, 1926

(See also *Christianity, God*)

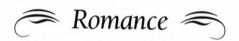

Romance

In real love you want the other person's good. In romantic love, you want the other person.

— MARGARET ANDERSON,
The Fiery Foundation, 1953

Men are so romantic, don't you think? They look for a perfect partner when what they should be looking for is perfect love.

— FAY WELDON,
Sunday Times, September 6, 1987

When one is in love, one always begins by deceiving oneself, and one always ends by deceiving others. That is what the world calls a romance.

—OSCAR WILDE,
The Picture of Dorian Gray, 1891

I used to think romantic love was a neurosis shared by two, a supreme foolishness. I no longer thought that. There's nothing foolish in loving anyone. Thinking you'll be loved in return is what's foolish.

—RITA MAE BROWN,
Bingo, 1988

Romantic love has always seemed to me unaccountable, unassailable, unforgettable, and nearly always unattainable.

—MARGARET ANDERSON,
The Fiery Fountains, 1953

And what's romance? Usually, a nice little tale where you have everything As You Like It, where rain never wets your jacket and gnats never bite your nose and it's always daisy-time.

—D. H. LAWRENCE,
Studies in Classic American Literature, 1924

A romantic man often feels more uplifted with two women than with one: his love seems to hit the ideal mark somewhere between two different faces.

—ELIZABETH BOWEN,
The Death of the Heart, 1938

(See also *Courtship, Enduring Love, Falling in Love, First Love, Foolish Love, Forbidden Love, Free Love, Great Love, Heart, Honeymoon, Kisses, Love, Loving, Marriage, Mature Love, May-December Romance, Memories of Love, True Love, Young Love*)

 *Sacrifice*

But you must believe me when I tell you that I have found it impossible to carry the heavy burden of responsibility and to discharge my duties as King as I would wish to do, without the help and support of the woman I love.

━EDWARD VIII,
   abdication speech, December 11, 1936

 *Scandal*

The scandal is often worse than the sin itself.

━MARGUERITE D'ANGOULEME,
   Heptameron, 1558

Love and scandal are the best sweeteners of tea.

━HENRY FIELDING,
   Love in Several Masques, 1743

(See also *Gossip*)

Seasons

O! How this spring of love resembleth
The uncertain glory of an April day.

— WILLIAM SHAKESPEARE,
The Two Gentlemen of Verona, 1592

Men are April when they woo, December when they wed; maids are May when they are maids, but the sky changes when they are wives.

— WILLIAM SHAKESPEARE,
As You Like It, 1599

Never hath absence been more grievous to me than this. To spend the month of April far from one's beloved, 'tis not to live at all.

— HENRY IV OF NAVARRE,
letter to Gabrielle d'Estrees

But I miss you most of all my darling
When autumn leaves start to fall.

— JOHNNY MERCER,
"Autumn Leaves," 1947

In the spring a livelier iris changes on the burnished dove
In the spring a young man's fancy lightly turns to thoughts of love.

— ALFRED, LORD TENNYSON,
"Locksley Hall," 1842

A man has every season, while a woman has only the right to spring.

— JANE FONDA,
Daily Mail, September 13, 1989

For like as herbs and trees bringeth forth fruit and flourish in May, in likewise every lusty heart that is in any manner a lover, springeth and flourisheth in lusty deeds.

    ━THOMAS MALORY,
      Le Morte d'Arthur, 1485

Every year, in the fulness o' summer, when the sukebind hangs heavy from the wains...'tes the same. And when the spring comes her house is upon her again. 'Tes the hand of Nature and we women cannot escape it.

    ━STELLA GIBBONS,
      Cold Comfort Farm, 1932

Secrets

Love ceases to be a pleasure, when it ceases to be a secret.

    ━APHRA BEHN,
      "The Lover's Watch," *Four O'Clock*, 1686

Your love to me was like an unread book . . .

    ━COUNTEE CULLEN,
      "Bright Bindings," *The Black Christ and Other Poems*, 1929

If a man cannot keep a measly affair secret, what is he doing in charge of the Intelligence Service?

    ━FREDERICK FORSYTH,
      on the breakup of the marriage of Foreign Secretary Robin
        Cook,
      Guardian, January 14, 1998

I doubt whether any girl would be satisfied with her lover's mind if she knew the whole of it.

    ━ANTHONY TROLLOPE,
      The Small House at Allington, 1864

Second Marriages

When a woman marries again it is because she detested her first husband. When a man marries again it is because he adored his first wife. Women try their luck; men risk theirs.

—OSCAR WILDE,
The Picture of Dorian Gray, 1891

Anyone who marries three girls from St. Louis hasn't learned much.

—GERTRUDE STEIN,
of Ernest Hemingway,
quoted in *Charmed Circle: Gertrude Stein and Company* by
J. R. Mellow, 1974

He loves his bonds, who when the first are broke,
Submits his neck unto a second yoke.

—ROBERT HERRICK,
"To Love," 1648

There are moments when the meanest of women may feel a sisterly sympathy for her husband's first wife.

—HELEN ROWLAND,
Reflections of a Bachelor Girl, 1903

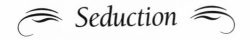

Seduction

A gentleman doesn't pounce...he glides

—QUENTIN CRISP,
Manners from Heaven, 1984

Seduction is often difficult to distinguish from rape. In seduction, the rapist bothers to buy a bottle of wine.
—ANDREA DWORKIN,
Letters from a War Zone, 1988

(See also *Romance, Sensuality, Sex, Sexuality*)

 *Self-Esteem*

We cease loving ourselves when no one loves us.
—MME. DE STÄEL,
Portraits of Women, 1891

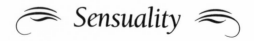 *Sensuality*

The Summer hath his joys,
And Winter his delights.
Though Love and all his pleasures are but toys,
They shorten tedious nights.
—THOMAS CAMPION,
"Now Winter Nights Enlarge," 1617

I have gone marking the blank atlas of your body
with crosses of fire.
My mouth went across; a spider, trying to hide.
In you, behind you, timid, driven by thirst.
—PABLO NERUDA,
"I Have Gone Marking," 1924

i like my body when it is with your
body. It is so quite new a thing.
Muscles better and nerves more.
i like your body. i like what it does,
i like its hows.

➤ E. E. CUMMINGS,
Sonnets-Actualities no. 8, 1925

Between her breasts is my home, between her breasts.
Three sides set on me space and fear, but the fourth side rests
Sure and a tower of strength, 'twixt the walls of her breasts.

➤ D. H. LAWRENCE,
"**The Time I've Lost in Wooing**," 1807

(See also *Romance, Sensuality, Sex, Sexuality*)

 *Sex*

The day after that wedding night I found that a distance of a thousand miles, abyss and discovery and irremediable metamorphosis,
separated me from the day before.

➤ COLETTE,
Noces, 1945

The ability to make love frivolously is the thing that distinguishes
human beings from beasts.

➤ HEYWOOD C. BROUN,
quoted in *The Algonquin Wits* by Robert E. Drennan, 1968

The only door into her bedroom led through the church.

➤ FRANCES PARKINSON KEYES,
Dinner at Antoines, 1948

It doesn't matter what you do in the bedroom as long as you don't do it in the street and frighten the horses.
> —MRS. PATRICK CAMPBELL,
>   quoted in *The Duchess of Jermyn Street* by Daphne Fielding

Women complain about sex more often than men. Their gripes fall into two major categories: (1) Not enough. (2) Too much.
> —ANN LANDERS,
>   *Truth Is Stranger*, 1968

Heaven and earth! How is it that bodies join but never meet?
> —BEAH RICHARDS,
>   "It's Time for Love," *A Black Woman Speaks and Other Poems*,
>   1974

The Englishman can get along with sex quite perfectly so long as he can pretend that it isn't sex but something else.
> —JAMES AGATE,
>   quoted in *The Selective Ego* by Tim Beaumont, ed., 1976

A sex symbol becomes a thing. I hate being a thing.
> —MARILYN MONROE,
>   quoted in *Uncommon Scold* by Abby Adams, 1989

Of the delights of this world man cares most for sexual intercourse. He will go to any lengths for it—risk fortune, character, reputation, life itself. And what do you think he has done? In a thousand years you would never guess—*He has left it out of his heaven!*
> —MARK TWAIN,
>   *Notebooks*, 1935

While we think of it, and talk of it
Let us leave it alone, physically, keep apart.
For while we have sex in the mind, we truly have none in the body.
> —D. H. LAWRENCE,
>   "Leave Sex Alone," 1929

Post coitum omne animal triste.
After coition every animal is sad.

—ANONYMOUS

You musn't force sex to do the work of love, or love to do the work of sex.

—MARY MCCARTHY,
The Group, 1954

Nobody dies from lack of sex. It's lack of love we die from.

—MARGARET ATWOOD,
The Handmaid's Tale, 1985

Plenty of guys are good at sex, but conversation, now there's an art.

—LINDA BARNES,
A Trouble of Fools, 1987

Sex is the tabasco sauce which an adolescent national palate sprinkles on every course in the menu.

—MARY DAY WINN,
Adam's Rib, 1931

There is nothing safe about sex. Their never will be.

—NORMAN MAILER,
International Herald Tribune, January 24, 1992

may i feel said he
(i'll squeal said she
just once said he)
it's fun said she
(may i touch said he
how much said she
a lot said he)
why not said she

—E. E. CUMMINGS,
Complete Poems, 1935

I could be content that we might procreate like trees, without conjunction, or that there were any way to perpetuate the world without this trivial and vulgar way of coition; it is the foolishest act a wise man commits in all his life.

    ⟵ SIR THOMAS BROWNE,
      Religio Medici, 1643

(See also *Seduction, Sensuality, Sexuality*)

 *Sexuality*

When she raises her eyelids, it's as if she were taking off her clothes.

    ⟵ COLETTE,
      Claudine and Annie, 1903

Sex appeal is 50% what you've got and 50% what people think you've got.

    ⟵ SOPHIA LOREN,
      quoted in *Halliwell's Filmgoer's Companion* by Leslie Halliwell, 1984

He was the kind of guy who could kiss you behind your ear and make you feel like you'd just had kinky sex.

    ⟵ JULIA ALVAREZ,
      How the Garcia Girls Lost Their Accents, 1991

This is the female form,
A divine nimbus exhales from it from head to foot,
It attracts with fierce undeniable attraction

    ⟵ WALT WHITMAN,
      Leaves of Grass, 1850

Pursuit and seduction are the essence of sexuality. It's part of the sizzle.

— CAMILLE LA PAGLIA,
   Playboy, October 1991

The contemplation of the erotic is a joyous frame in life's rich comic strip.

— STEPHEN FRY,
   Tatler, December 1986

He kissed me under the Moorish wall and I thought well as well him as another and then I asked him with my eyes to ask again yes and then he asked me would I yes to say yes my mountain flower and first i put my arms around him yes and drew him down to me so he could feel my breasts all perfume yes and his heart was going like mad and yes I said yes I will Yes

— JAMES JOYCE,
   Ulysses, 1922

She gave me a smile I could feel in my hip pocket.

— RAYMOND CHANDLER,
   Farewell, My Lovely, 1940

(See also *Seduction, Sensuality, Sex*)

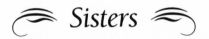 *Sisters*

Never praise a sister to a sister, in the hope of your compliments reaching the proper ears, and so preparing the way for you later on. Sisters are women first, and sisters afterwards.

— RUDYARD KIPLING,
   Plain Tales from the Hills, 1888

But I kissed her little sister
And forgot my Clementine
    ➤ PERCY MONTROSE,
        "Clementine," 1884

If only I hadn't had sisters
How much more romantic I'd be
But my sisters were such little blisters
that all women are sisters to me.
    ➤ JUSTIN RICHARDSON,
        "Sisters," 1949

(See also *Family*)

 *Sleep*

But be, as you have been, my happiness;
Let me sleep beside you each night, like a spoon;
When, starting from my dreams, I groan to you,
May your "I love you" send me back to sleep.
    ➤ RANDALL JARRELL,
        "Woman," 1966

Sleeping as quiet as death, side by wrinkled side, toothless, salt and brown, like two old kippers in a box.
    ➤ DYLAN THOMAS,
        Under Milk Wood, 1954

Husband, I sleep with you every night
And like it; but each morning when I wake
I've dreamed of my first love, the subtle serpent
    ➤ RANDALL JARRELL,
        in *Nature There Is Neither Right nor Left nor Wrong*

Smile

That grin! She could have taken it off her face and put it on the table.

—Jean Stafford,
Bad Characters, 1954

(See also *Contentment, Happiness*)

Support

To keep a lamp burning we have to keep putting oil in it.

—Mother Teresa,
Time, December 29, 1975

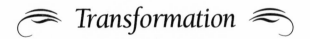

Transformation

Love makes cottages manors, and straw into silken ribbons.

—Estonian proverb

Love looks through spectacles that make copper appear gold, poverty like riches, and tears like pearls.

—Peruvian proverb

True Love

The course of true love never did run smooth.
— WILLIAM SHAKESPEARE,
A Midsummer Night's Dream, 1596

True love is like ghosts, which everyone talks about but few have seen.
— DUC DE LA ROCHEFOUCAULD,
Maximes, 1678

True love comes quietly, without banners or flashing lights. If you hear bells, get your ears checked.
— ERICH SEGAL,
quoted in *Words of Wisdom* by William Safire and Leonard
Safire, 1989

(See also *Enduring Love, Falling in Love, First Love, Foolish Love, Forbidden Love, Free Love, Love, Love at First Sight, Loving, Memories of Love, Unrequited Love, Young Love*)

Trust

How desperately we wish to maintain our trust in those we love! In the face of everything, we try to find reasons to trust. Because losing faith is worse than falling out of love.
— SONIA JOHNSON,
From Housewife to Heretic, 1981

He who has trusted where he ought not will surely mistrust where he ought not.
↙MARIE VON EBNER-ESCHENBACH,
Aphorisms, 1893

How can the people trust the harvest unless they see it sown?
↙MARY RENAULT,
The King Must Die, 1958

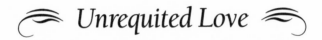 *Unrequited Love*

Love clamors far more incessantly and passionately at a closed gate than an open one!
↙MARIE CORELLI,
The Master Christian, 1900

To love somebody
Who doesn't love you
Is like going to a temple
And worshipping the behind
Of a wooden statue
Of a hungry devil.
↙LADY KASA,
quoted in *Women Poets of the World* by Joanna Bankier and Deirdre Lashgari, eds., 1983

There's nothing like unrequited love to take all the taste out of a peanut butter sandwich.
↙CHARLES SCHULZ,
Peanuts

Loving one who does not love you is loving the rain that falls in the forest.

⮌Old Kenyan proverb

The love that lasts longest is the love that is never returned.

⮌SOMERSET MAUGHAM,
recalled on his death, December 16, 1965

(See also *Blind Love, Changeable Love, End of Love, Falling in Love, First Love, Foolish Love, Forbidden Love, Great Love, Heartbreak, Love, Memories of Love, Painful Love*)

Wine

Fill ev'ry glass, for wine inspires us,
And fires us
With courage, love and joy.
Women and wine should life employ.
Is there aught else on earth desirous?

⮌JOHN GAY,
The Beggar's Opera, 1728

(See also *Cooking, Food*)

 Wives

I chose my wife, as she did her wedding gown, not for a fine glossy surface, but such qualities as would wear well.

— OLIVER GOLDSMITH,
The Vicar of Wakefield, 1766

Wives are young men's mistresses, companions for middle age, and old men's nurses.

— FRANCIS BACON,
Of Marriage and Single Life, Essays, 1625

A little house well filled, a little field well tilled, and a little wife well willed, are great riches.

— BENJAMIN FRANKLIN,
Poor Richard's Almanac, 1735

She is a winsome wee thing,
She is a handsome wee thing,
She is a lo'esome wee thing,
This sweet wee wife o' mine.

— ROBERT BURNS,
"My Wife's a Winsome Wee Thing," 1792

House and wealth are inherited from our fathers, but a sensible wife is a gift from the Lord.

— Proverbs 19:14

(See also *Engagement, Husbands, Marriage*)

Women

Nature has given women so much power that the law has very wisely given them little.

➤ SAMUEL JOHNSON,
letter to John Taylor, August 18, 1763

A woman who is loved always has success.

➤ VICKI BAUM,
Grand Hotel, 1929

I think women need kindness more than love.

➤ ALICE CHILDRESS,
"Alice Childress," in *Interviews with Contemporary Women
Playwrights* by Kathleen Betsko and Rachel Koenig, 1987

Women like not only to conquer, but to be conquered.

➤ WILLIAM MAKEPEACE THACKERAY,
The Virginians, 1859

Handle with care: women, glass and love.

➤ Swedish proverb

(See also *Marriage, Men, Wives, Women vs. Men*)

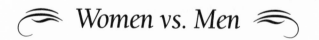

Women vs. Men

We all marry strangers. All men are strangers to all women.

➤ MARY HEATON VORSE,
"The Pink Fence," *McCall's*, 1920

A woman is a foreign land,
Of which, though there he settle young,
A man will ne'er quire understand
The customs, politics, and tongue
— COVENTRY PATMORE,
"The Angel in the House," 1856

A man falls in love through his eyes, a woman through her imagination, and then they both speak of it as an affair of "the heart."
— HELEN ROWLAND,
A Guide to Men, 1922

It is strange what a man may do, and a woman yet think him an angel.
— WILLIAM MAKEPEACE THACKERAY,
Henry Esmond, 1852

In revenge and in love woman is more barbarous than man.
— FRIEDRICH WILHELM NIETZSCHE,
Beyond Good and Evil, 1886

Men are like the earth and we are the moon; we turn always one side to them, and they think there is no other, because they don't see it—but there is.
— OLIVE EMILY SCHREINER,
The Story of an African Farm, 1883

The basic discovery about any people is the discovery of the relationship between its men and women.
— PEARL S. BUCK,
Of Men and Women, 1941

It is only rarely that one can see in a little boy the promise of a man, but one can almost always see in a little girl the threat of a woman.
— ALEXANDRE DUMAS,
attributed remark, 1895

Here's how men think. Sex, work—and those are reversible, depending on age—sex, work, food, sports and lastly, begrudgingly, relationships. And here's how women think. Relationships, relationships, relationships, work, sex, shopping, weight, food.
>—CARRIE FISHER,
>*Surrender the Pink*, 1990

Man's love is of man's life a thing apart,
'Tis woman's whole existence.
>—LORD BYRON,
>*Don Juan*, 1819

I expect that Woman will be the last thing civilized by Man.
>—GEORGE MEREDITH,
>*The Ordeal of Richard Feberel*, 1859

We are becoming the men we wanted to marry.
>—GLORIA STEINEM,
>*Ms.*, 1982

What is most beautiful in virile men is something feminine; what is most beautiful in feminine women is something masculine.
>—SUSAN SONTAG,
>*Against Interpretation*, 1966

If men knew how women pass the time when they are alone, they'd never marry.
>—O. HENRY,
>*Four Million*, 1906

Women are programmed to love completely, and men are programmed to spread it around.
>—BERYL BAINBRIDGE,
>*Daily Telegraph*, September 10, 1996

Women are really much nicer than men:
No wonder we like them.
>—KINGSLEY AMIS,
>*A Bookshop Idyll*, 1956

Man dreams of fame while woman wakes to love.

─ALFRED, LORD TENNYSON,
Idylls of the King, 1859

(See also *Men,Women*)

 *World*

I was in love with the whole world and all that lived in its rainy arms

─LOUISE ERDRICH,
Love Medicine, 1984

Earth's the right place for love;
I don't know where it's likely to go better.

─ROBERT FROST,
"Birches," 1920

 *Young Love*

Youth's the season made for joys,
Love is then our duty.

─JOHN GAY,
The Beggar's Opera, 1728

I thought that spring must last forevermore
For I was young and loved, and it was May.

─VERA BRITTAIN,
Poems of the War and After, 1934

No, there's nothing half so sweet in life
As love's young dream.

➤ THOMAS MOORE,
Irish Melodies, 1834

This bud of love, by summer's ripening breath,
May prove a beauteous flower when next we meet.

➤ WILLIAM SHAKESPEARE,
Romeo and Juliet, 1596

(See also *Blind Love, Changeable Love, Enduring Love, Falling in Love, First Love, Foolish Love, Forbidden Love, Free Love, Heartbreak, Love, Love at First Sight, Loving, Mature Love, Memories of Love, Painful Love, True Love, Unrequited Love*)

Index